I0844503

SMALL SCALE, BIG IMPACT: DIGITAL TRANSFORMATION ROADMAP FOR SMALL AND MEDIUM-SIZED BUSINESSES

SAJU JOSEPH

Table of Contents

1. Introduction: The New Digital Age for SMBs

2. Understanding Today's Digital Landscape

3. The Basics: Must-Have Technologies for Every SMB

4. Mastering Digital Marketing

About the Author

Getting to this pivotal point in my life has been long and arduous. However, I am mindful that this journey is the beginning of what lies ahead. Bearing witness to the remarkable and awe-inspiring evolution of the digital landscape throughout my lifespan has been an enthralling and captivating experience.

My journey started as a confused computer science engineering graduate, unsure of what to pursue next—I landed a job at a startup digital agency in Mumbai, where I initially did data entry for an e-commerce website in the UK. Eventually, I learned about digital marketing and started applying my knowledge to small and big projects, leading teams and climbing the corporate ladder. It's like fixing nuts and bolts like a young mechanic on his way to becoming a skilled car mechanic someday.

Today, I hold certifications as an AI Business Leader & Customer Engagement Engineer. With 18 years of experience, I have worked with leading brands in the banking, retail, real estate, beauty, and manufacturing sectors. I have assisted these sectors in building digital engagement platforms and implementing growth-oriented digital strategies. I am also proud to lead two forward-thinking businesses - an offshore technology company that continually pushes the limits of what can be accomplished in the digital realm and an innovative digital agency specializing in cutting-edge creative solutions.

Through these ventures, I have had the incredible opportunity to witness firsthand the immense potential of combining technology with creativity. By harnessing the power of both, I have been able to carve a unique and influential niche in the entrepreneurial landscape, constantly striving to stay ahead of the curve and deliver exceptional results to our clients.

I am also a certified business coach, committed to guiding and empowering fellow entrepreneurs on their journeys to success. I wrote this book to offer a roadmap for digital transformation to small and medium-sized companies and fellow founders, helping them harness technological advancements and create a meaningful impact.

- Saju Joseph

INTRODUCTION: THE NEW DIGITAL AGE FOR SMBS

Brief about the digital transformation wave

The digital transformation wave, often called "digital transformation," is a fundamental concept in today's business landscape. It represents a profound shift in how businesses operate, brought about by the rapid advancements in technology and the ever-changing expectations of consumers. Understanding that the digital transformation wave is far more than just a trendy buzzword is crucial. It encompasses a wide range of activities aimed at integrating digital technologies into every facet of a business. This comprehensive approach leads to substantial and fundamental changes in how the company operates and ultimately delivers value to its customers.

The Genesis of the Digital Transformation Wave

The digital age can be traced back to the rise of personal computers in the 1980s. Still, the true momentum for digital transformation began with the widespread adoption of the internet in the 1990s and early 2000s. The Internet revolutionized communication, information dissemination, and commerce.

The next significant leap came with the proliferation of smartphones and mobile devices, which brought about an era of omnipresent connectivity. Suddenly, consumers had access to the world at their fingertips, and businesses had to evolve rapidly.

In the early days of digital transformation, Amazon and Netflix greatly benefited from embracing digital technologies.

Initially an online bookstore, Amazon saw the potential of the internet and transformed itself into the world's largest online marketplace. Amazon revolutionized the retail industry using digital technologies like advanced recommendation algorithms and efficient supply chain management systems. The company's ability to provide a wide range of products, personalized shopping experiences, and fast, reliable delivery has made it a dominant force in e-commerce.

Initially a DVD rental service, Netflix underwent a remarkable digital transformation that disrupted the traditional video rental industry. By shifting its focus from physical media to digital streaming, Netflix took advantage of high-speed internet's growing popularity and video compression technology advancements. The company's seamless user experience, personalized recommendations, and original content production have positioned it as a global leader in the entertainment industry.

Amazon and Netflix recognized the changing landscape and used digital technologies to redefine their business models. They survived and thrived in an increasingly digital world by embracing digital transformation.

Key Drivers of the Transformation

Several factors have driven the relentless pace of digital transformation:

1. **Technological Advancements**: Innovations such as cloud computing, artificial intelligence, big data analytics, and the Internet of Things (IoT) have provided businesses with tools that were previously unimaginable.
2. **Changing Consumer Behavior**: Modern consumers expect instant, on-the-go services. They prioritize personalized experiences and seamless digital interactions with businesses.
3. **Globalization**: The digital era has significantly reduced the size of the world, allowing businesses to operate and compete globally.
4. **Agility and Innovation**: In today's fast-paced digital world, adapting and innovating quickly has become a competitive advantage.

Impact on Businesses

Digital transformation has impacted every industry, including healthcare, finance, retail, and entertainment. Its impact can be summarized in several key areas:

- **Operational Efficiency**: Automated processes, data analytics, and digital tools streamline operations, reduce costs, and enhance productivity.
- **Customer Engagement**: Digital platforms enable businesses to engage with customers quickly, cultivate loyalty, and enhance user experiences.
- **Innovation**: New technologies pave the way for innovative products, services, and business models.

- **Data-Driven Decision Making**: With abundant data, businesses can make better-informed decisions, predict market trends, and gain insights into customer behaviors.

Challenges and Considerations

The digital transformation wave brings both opportunities and challenges. Businesses face hurdles such as cybersecurity concerns, data privacy issues, and the need to upskill the workforce continuously. Furthermore, digital transformation is not solely about implementing new technologies; it also involves changing the organizational culture, mindset, and underlying business processes.

The Road Ahead

As we progress through the 21st century, the wave of digital transformation is anticipated to persist. Newer technologies such as quantum computing, augmented reality, and blockchain are set to redefine the business landscape even further. To stay ahead of the curve, businesses must be adaptable, forward-thinking, and dedicated to continuous learning and innovation.

In conclusion, the digital transformation wave represents a passing trend and a fundamental shift in the business paradigm. Embracing it is no longer optional but necessary for businesses striving to thrive in this digital age.

The importance of SMBs in the economy

Small and Medium-sized Businesses (SMBs), often referred to as the backbone of many economies, play a crucial role in fostering innovation, creating jobs, and promoting economic growth. Although they may appear modest compared to multinational conglomerates, their combined influence on the national and global economy is significant. This chapter explores the diverse ways in which SMBs contribute to and strengthen the economy.

1. Employment Generation

Local Job Creation: Small and medium-sized businesses (SMBs) are crucial as employers in most economies. Whether it is a local store, a mid-sized technology firm, or a budding startup, these businesses create jobs for a large portion of the population. Often, these jobs are concentrated in specific areas, providing livelihoods for millions of people.

Diverse Opportunities: Small and medium-sized businesses (SMBs) often provide various job opportunities across different functions, including entry-level and managerial positions. This is in contrast to large enterprises that may have more specialized roles.

One example of an Indian small business that has created local job opportunities is "Chai Point." Chai Point is a popular chain of tea outlets in India that serves freshly brewed tea. With numerous outlets across various cities, Chai Point has created employment opportunities for many individuals, ranging from tea makers and servers to store managers and administrative staff. The business has provided jobs and contributed to the local economy by sourcing ingredients from local suppliers and engaging with the community.

2. Innovation and Niche Market Exploration

Pioneering New Markets: Small and medium-sized businesses (SMBs) are agile due to their size. They have the flexibility to explore niche markets or create new ones. This often results in the developing of novel products and services that large corporations might overlook.

Rapid Adaptation: With fewer bureaucratic layers, small and medium-sized businesses (SMBs) can adapt quickly to market changes, technological advancements, and customer feedback. This allows them to drive innovation at a faster rate.

One notable example of an Indian company that achieved growth through innovation and niche market exploration is "Zomato." Initially starting as a restaurant discovery and food delivery platform in India, Zomato has expanded globally. The company took advantage of the rising trend of online food ordering. It used technology to create a user-friendly platform connecting users with various restaurants and food options.

Zomato's innovative approach, combined with its focus on localized services, allowed it to cater to the diverse culinary preferences of Indian consumers. The company explored niche markets by introducing features such as online menu listings, user reviews, and food delivery services, which were relatively new concepts in the Indian market then.

Through continuous innovation and adaptation to customer needs, Zomato successfully established itself as a leader in the food technology industry. It has become one of India's top online food delivery platforms, expanding its services to multiple countries and attracting substantial investments.

Zomato's success story inspires other Indian startups and highlights the potential for growth and achievement through innovation and niche market exploration in the Indian business landscape.

3. Boosting Local Economies

Community Engagement: Small and medium-sized businesses (SMBs) often have strong community connections. They prioritize buying from local suppliers, hiring local employees, and actively participating in local issues. This helps to keep money circulating within the community, leading to its growth and development.

Local Supply Chains: Frequently, they depend on local suppliers and service providers, which helps support nearby businesses and creates an interconnected web of economic activity.

One notable example of an Indian company that has boosted local economies is "Fabindia." Fabindia is a well-known Indian retail chain specializing in handmade products, including clothing, home furnishings, and accessories. The company collaborates closely with artisans and craftspeople from rural India, supporting their traditional craftsmanship and providing sustainable livelihoods.

By sourcing directly from artisans and promoting their products, Fabindia ensures fair wages and helps preserve cultural heritage. The company's commitment to supporting local artisans has significantly impacted rural economies, particularly in regions where traditional arts and crafts are prevalent.

Fabindia has created market access and visibility for numerous artisans and craftsmen through its extensive network of stores in India and international markets. By connecting rural artisans with urban consumers, Fabindia has opened up new economic opportunities and helped uplift local communities.

Fabindia's approach of blending traditional craftsmanship with contemporary designs has resonated with consumers who appreciate ethically sourced and handcrafted products. The company's success has benefited the artisans it works with and contributed to the overall growth of India's handicraft industry.

Fabindia's model of promoting local artisans and their crafts is an inspiring example of how a business can positively impact local economies by preserving traditional skills, supporting communities, and fostering sustainable economic development.

4. Enhancing Competition and Consumer Choice

Diverse Offerings: Small and medium-sized businesses (SMBs) expand the variety of consumer products and services. This helps ensure competitive prices and fosters innovation.

Personalized Services: Their localized operations often enable a deeper understanding of their customer base, resulting in tailored offerings and high customer satisfaction.

One remarkable example of an Indian company that enhanced competition and consumer choice is "Flipkart." Founded in 2007, Flipkart started as an online bookstore and later expanded into a full-fledged e-commerce platform. The company played a significant role in revolutionizing the Indian e-commerce industry and transforming how people shop there.

Flipkart introduced various products across various categories, including electronics, fashion, home appliances, and more. By offering competitive prices, attractive discounts, and a convenient shopping experience, Flipkart quickly gained popularity among Indian consumers.

The company's innovative approach, including features like cash-on-delivery, easy returns, and customer reviews, helped build trust and confidence among online shoppers. Flipkart's efforts to provide a seamless online shopping experience and a diverse selection of products enhanced competition in the Indian market.

Furthermore, Flipkart's success inspired the emergence of other e-commerce players in India, leading to increased competition and further expanding consumer choice. The company's impact on the Indian retail industry prompted traditional brick-and-mortar stores to adapt and embrace e-commerce, ultimately benefiting consumers with more options and competitive pricing.

Flipkart's journey from a small online bookstore to one of India's leading e-commerce giants demonstrates how an Indian company can disrupt the market, enhance competition, and provide consumers with a wide range of choices, ultimately shaping the retail landscape in the country.

5. Filling Market Gaps

Versatility: Small and medium-sized businesses (SMBs) have the advantage of catering to specific, often overlooked market segments. Whether offering artisanal products, specialized services, or meeting unique local demands, these businesses can fill the gaps left by more giant corporations.

Swiggy is an online food delivery platform that emerged in the Indian market to meet the increasing demand for convenient and reliable food delivery services.

Before Swiggy's entry, traditional food delivery options were limited, often restricted to specific restaurants or offering limited menus. Swiggy identified this gap in the market and aimed to provide a wide range of food options from various restaurants, delivered directly to customer's doorsteps.

By leveraging technology, Swiggy developed a user-friendly platform that allowed customers to explore multiple restaurants, browse menus, place orders, and track deliveries in real-time. The company also optimized delivery logistics to ensure prompt and efficient service.

Swiggy's innovative approach and commitment to customer satisfaction quickly gained popularity among Indian consumers. The company's extensive network of delivery partners and collaborations with numerous restaurants enabled it to offer a diverse culinary experience to customers, providing convenience and choice.

Swiggy's success filled the market gap for reliable and efficient food delivery services and transformed how people in India order food. The company's disruptive model inspired the growth of the online food delivery industry, encouraging other players to enter the market and expanding consumer options.

Swiggy's story serves as an inspiring example of an Indian company that identified a market gap, utilized technology to bridge it, and successfully revolutionized the food delivery industry in India, enhancing convenience and delighting customers in the process.

6. Contribution to GDP

Small and medium-sized businesses (SMBs) may be small individually but significantly contribute to a country's Gross Domestic Product (GDP). The combined revenues, profits, and taxes generated by SMBs play a crucial role in strengthening national economic indicators.

Founded by Dhirubhai Ambani in 1966, Reliance Industries is a conglomerate with interests in various sectors, including petrochemicals, refining, oil, and telecommunications.

Reliance Industries has played a crucial role in India's economic growth and development. The company's contributions to the GDP are substantial, driven by its significant investments and operations across multiple industries. Reliance Industries has transformed India's petrochemical and refining sectors, driving innovation and creating employment opportunities on a large scale.

One of the company's flagship projects, the Reliance Jamnagar Refinery, stands as one of the world's largest refining complexes. It can process vast amounts of crude oil, contributing significantly to India's energy security and reducing its dependence on imported petroleum products.

In addition, Reliance Jio Infocomm Limited, a subsidiary of Reliance Industries, revolutionized India's telecommunications sector. With its affordable data plans and widespread network coverage, Reliance Jio played a crucial role in digital connectivity and adopting digital technologies nationwide. This, in turn, has had a profound impact on various sectors of the Indian economy, including e-commerce, digital payments, and online services.

Reliance Industries' investments and business operations have generated substantial revenues, profits, and taxes, significantly contributing to India's GDP. The success story of this company exemplifies how a single Indian company can substantially impact the national economy, driving growth and creating economic opportunities for millions of people.

The contributions of Reliance Industries to the GDP highlight the importance of large-scale businesses in India's economic landscape. They serve as engines of growth, attracting investments, creating jobs, and fostering innovation, ultimately strengthening the country's economic indicators.

7. Resilience During Economic Downturns

Diversified Risk: Small and medium-sized businesses (SMBs) can serve as an economic buffer due to their widespread presence across sectors and geographies. While specific sectors may encounter challenges, others may thrive, counterbalancing during economic downturns.

One inspiring example of an Indian company that showed resilience during an economic downturn is "Tata Consultancy Services" (TCS). TCS is a multinational information technology (IT) services and consulting company headquartered in Mumbai, India.

During the global financial crisis of 2008-2009, many businesses faced significant challenges and had to make tough decisions. However, TCS managed to navigate through the problem and emerge stronger.

One key factor that contributed to TCS's resilience was its diversified portfolio of clients and services. The company served clients across various industries and geographies, which helped mitigate the downturn's impact in specific sectors. Additionally, TCS firmly focused on innovation and digital transformation, positioning it well to adapt to changing market demands.

During the crisis, TCS continued to invest in research and development, enabling it to offer cutting-edge solutions and services to its clients. The company also focused on cost optimization and operational efficiency, ensuring competitiveness in a challenging market environment.

Furthermore, TCS leveraged its global delivery model to deliver services remotely and serve clients worldwide. This flexibility and ability to work remotely were crucial in maintaining business continuity during the economic downturn.

By demonstrating resilience, adaptability, and a customer-centric approach, TCS not only weathered the economic storm but continued to grow. The company's ability to provide value to its clients, invest in innovation, and navigate challenging times solidified its position as a leading player in the IT services industry.

TCS's success story during an economic downturn inspires other Indian companies, showcasing the importance of resilience, strategic planning, and a customer-centric approach to overcoming challenges and maintaining growth in a volatile business environment.

8. Fostering Entrepreneurial Spirit

Cultivating Skills and Leadership: Small and medium-sized businesses (SMBs) serve as breeding grounds for entrepreneurial skills. In these organizations, employees often have to take on multiple roles, which leads to developing a wide range of skills and fosters the growth of future business leaders.

Inspiring Others: The success stories of local businesses often encourage others in the community to start their entrepreneurial journeys. This perpetuates a cycle of innovation and economic activity.

OYO Rooms is a hospitality chain that originated in India and has since expanded globally. The company has revolutionized the concept of budget accommodation by bringing together and standardizing small, independent hotels under a single brand.

OYO Rooms provides a platform and support system for small hotel owners to join their network and improve their business operations. They offer training, technological solutions, and marketing support to empower these entrepreneurs. This not only helps the hotel owners enhance their services but also allows them to access a more extensive customer base.

Through their efforts, OYO Rooms has created new opportunities for small hotel owners to thrive in the hospitality industry. Many individuals who previously faced challenges in running their independent hotels have found success through the OYO Rooms platform. This enables them to grow their businesses while benefiting from OYO Rooms' brand recognition and operational support.

OYO Rooms' success in fostering entrepreneurship extends beyond India and has inspired individuals globally to explore similar business models. Their innovative approach and support system have transformed the budget accommodation sector and helped numerous entrepreneurs achieve their dreams of building successful hospitality businesses.

The story of OYO Rooms exemplifies how an Indian company can foster entrepreneurial spirit by providing aspiring entrepreneurs with a platform, resources, and mentorship. OYO Rooms has contributed to job creation, economic development, and innovation in the hospitality industry by empowering individuals to become business owners and supporting their growth.

OYO Rooms' model inspires other companies and highlights the potential for fostering entrepreneurial spirit as a catalyst for economic growth and empowerment in India and beyond.

Conclusion

Small and medium-sized businesses (SMBs) are more than just "small" businesses. They play a vital economic role by driving growth, fostering innovation, and building communities. Recognizing their significance is crucial for policymakers, investors, and the general public, as supporting SMBs strengthens the economy's foundation. Ensuring SMBs have the tools and resources to navigate this era successfully becomes essential as we enter the digital age.

The increasing relevance of technology for SMBs

Technology is no longer exclusive to large corporations with substantial resources in the digital age. Small and Medium-sized Businesses (SMBs) are quickly realizing technology's game-changing potential, considering it an essential element for growth, efficiency, and competitiveness. As we progress into the 21st century, the interdependent connection between SMBs and technology continues to develop, paving the way for a new era of business operations and opportunities.

1. Leveling the Playing Field

Democratizing Access: Technology, particularly cloud-based solutions, has made advanced tools and platforms more accessible and affordable for small and medium-sized businesses (SMBs). This democratization enables them to compete with larger entities in previously unimaginable ways.

Expanding Reach: Digital platforms allow small and medium-sized businesses (SMBs) to expand beyond local boundaries and reach national and global audiences with minimal additional costs.

An Indian company can level the playing field by democratizing access and expanding reach through technology. By embracing cloud-based solutions and digital platforms, the company can access advanced tools and platforms at affordable costs. This democratization allows the company to compete with larger entities on a more equal footing, enabling them to leverage technology in previously unimaginable ways.

Expanding reach is another crucial aspect. Through digital platforms, the Indian company can transcend local boundaries and reach national and global audiences with minimal additional costs. By establishing an online presence, such as a website and social media accounts, the company can engage with customers around the clock, providing information, support, and online purchasing options. This level of accessibility helps the company expand its customer base beyond traditional physical limitations and tap into new markets.

By democratizing access and expanding reach through technology, an Indian company can overcome resource constraints and compete with more giant corporations. This allows them to unlock growth opportunities, enhance efficiency, and establish a strong presence in the digital age.

2. Operational Efficiency and Cost Savings

Automation: Tools that automate repetitive tasks, such as invoicing, customer relationship management, and inventory tracking, help small and medium-sized businesses (SMBs) operate more efficiently and reduce manual errors.

Data-Driven Decisions: Analytical tools provide small and medium-sized businesses (SMBs) with insights from their data, allowing them to make informed decisions that were once only available to corporations with dedicated research teams.

Automation and data-driven decisions can significantly improve operational efficiency and cost savings for an Indian company. The company can streamline repetitive tasks and minimize manual errors by utilizing automation tools for invoicing, customer relationship management, and inventory tracking. This allows employees to focus on more strategic and value-added activities, ultimately enhancing productivity and efficiency.

Furthermore, implementing data-driven decision-making processes empowers the Indian company to make informed choices based on insights derived from their data. Analytical tools enable them to analyze customer behavior, market trends, and operational metrics to identify areas for improvement and optimization. By making data-driven decisions, the company can allocate resources more effectively, optimize processes, and identify opportunities to save costs.

For instance, the Indian company can automate the invoicing process, reducing the time and effort required to generate and send invoices. This saves time and minimizes the risk of errors and delays. Additionally, by analyzing customer data and purchase patterns, the company can identify cost-saving opportunities, such as optimizing inventory levels to minimize carrying costs or identifying areas of operational inefficiency to streamline processes and reduce waste.

By embracing automation and data-driven decisions, an Indian company can enhance operational efficiency, reduce costs, and gain a competitive advantage in the digital age.

3. Enhancing Customer Engagement and Experience

Digital Presence: Websites, social media, and e-commerce platforms enable small and medium-sized businesses (SMBs) to interact with customers 24/7. They offer information, support, and online purchasing options.

Personalization: Technology empowers businesses to customize customer experiences, from personalized email campaigns to product recommendations. This enhances customer loyalty and satisfaction.

Firstly, establishing a solid digital presence through a website, social media platforms, and e-commerce channels enables the Indian company to interact with customers around the clock. They can provide valuable information, offer customer support, and help with online purchasing options. This availability allows customers to engage with the company at their convenience, fostering a positive and seamless customer experience.

Secondly, personalization plays a crucial role in enhancing customer engagement. By utilizing technology, the Indian company can customize experiences for individual customers. This can include personalized email campaigns that address customers by name or offering tailored product recommendations based on their previous purchases or browsing history. Through personalization, the company can create a sense of exclusivity and make customers feel valued, ultimately leading to increased loyalty and satisfaction.

For example, the Indian company can implement a personalized email campaign that addresses each customer by name and offers exclusive discounts or promotions based on their preferences. This targeted approach makes customers feel recognized and appreciated, enhancing their engagement and overall experience with the company.

By leveraging their digital presence and implementing personalization strategies, an Indian company can establish meaningful connections with their customers, provide tailored experiences, and drive customer engagement and satisfaction to new heights.

4. Expanding Product and Service Offerings

Digital Products: Small and medium-sized businesses (SMBs) can explore the creation of digital products or platforms, such as online courses or apps, to access additional sources of revenue.

Service Diversification: With digital tools, small and medium-sized businesses (SMBs) can provide value-added services such as online consultations, virtual tours, or digital memberships.

For example, companies can develop online courses, e-books, or mobile applications related to their industry expertise. By leveraging their knowledge and expertise, they can provide valuable digital products that cater to a broader audience beyond their local market.

With the help of digital tools, the Indian SMB can provide value-added services online. They can offer customers online consultations, virtual tours, or digital memberships. For instance, a fitness studio can provide virtual classes or personalized online training programs. By diversifying their services digitally, they can reach a broader customer base and tap into new revenue streams.

By embracing digital products and service diversification, an Indian SMB can expand its offerings beyond traditional physical limitations.

They can leverage their expertise and creativity to develop digital products that cater to a global audience. Additionally, by diversifying their services and providing online experiences, they can reach customers beyond their local market and create new revenue opportunities. This approach allows the Indian SMB to adapt to the digital age, stay competitive, and unlock growth potential.

5. Fostering Innovation

Rapid Prototyping: Technologies like 3D printing enable businesses to rapidly and cost-effectively iterate product designs.

Collaborative Tools: Platforms facilitating remote work and collaboration can help small and medium-sized businesses (SMBs) access talent and expertise worldwide.

Rapid prototyping, made possible by technologies like 3D printing, enables companies to iterate and refine product designs quickly. By creating cost-effective and timely physical prototypes, Indian companies can gather valuable feedback, identify improvements, and accelerate development. Rapid prototyping allows companies to test ideas, validate concepts, and bring products to market faster, fostering a culture of innovation.

In addition, collaborative tools facilitate remote work and collaboration, enabling Indian companies to access talent and expertise worldwide. These tools provide a platform for team members to collaborate, share ideas, and work together on projects regardless of geographical barriers. By leveraging collaborative tools, Indian companies can tap into diverse knowledge and perspectives, fostering a collaborative and innovative environment. Furthermore, these tools promote efficient communication, streamline workflows, and enhance productivity, driving organizational innovation.

By embracing rapid prototyping and utilizing collaborative tools, Indian companies can cultivate a culture of innovation, nurture creativity, and drive forward-thinking initiatives. These approaches enable companies to quickly iterate and refine their products, leverage global talent, and stay ahead of the curve in a rapidly evolving business landscape.

6. Enhancing Scalability

Cloud Solutions: Cloud platforms can scale with the business, eliminating the need for significant upfront investments in infrastructure.

Cloud platforms offer scalability that can align with a company's growth trajectory. By utilizing cloud-based services, an Indian company can avoid the need for significant upfront investments in infrastructure. Instead, they can use the pay-as-you-go model and adjust their resources based on demand. As the company expands, it can quickly scale its cloud resources to handle increased traffic, data storage, and computing power. This flexibility enables the Indian company to efficiently scale its operations without requiring significant hardware investments or infrastructure upgrades.

Digital Marketing: With their pay-as-you-go models, online advertising platforms enable small and medium-sized businesses (SMBs) to adjust their marketing efforts according to budget and response.

Digital marketing offers a scalable approach to reach a wider audience and grow a company's customer base. Indian companies can leverage online advertising platforms to customize their marketing efforts based on budget and response. They can start with a smaller marketing budget and gradually increase it as they see positive results. Digital marketing channels, such as social media advertising, search engine marketing, and content marketing, provide precise targeting options, enabling Indian companies to reach their desired audience effectively. Companies can optimize their campaigns and improve scalability by analyzing performance metrics and adjusting marketing strategies accordingly.

By utilizing cloud solutions and digital marketing, an Indian company can improve scalability by effectively managing resources, expanding its reach, and targeting a broader audience. This approach allows the company to adapt to evolving business needs, accommodate growth, and seize cost-effective new opportunities.

7. Strengthening Security and Trust

Cybersecurity: Advanced cybersecurity tools, once only affordable for large enterprises, are now accessible to SMBs. These tools provide data protection and help build customer trust.

Implementing advanced cybersecurity tools and practices is crucial for an Indian company to strengthen security and build customer trust. The company can protect its sensitive data, intellectual property, and customer information from cyber threats and attacks by investing in cybersecurity measures. This includes implementing firewalls, antivirus software, and encryption protocols and conducting regular security audits to identify and mitigate vulnerabilities. By prioritizing cybersecurity, the company demonstrates its commitment to protecting customer data and maintaining a secure online environment.

Digital Payments: Secure online payment gateways enable small and medium-sized businesses (SMBs) to provide customers with multiple payment options, improving transaction safety and convenience.

Offering secure online payment options is a way for an Indian company to enhance security and trust. By partnering with reputable payment gateways and implementing secure online payment systems, the company can provide customers with a safe and convenient way to transact. Secure payment gateways use encryption and fraud detection mechanisms to protect sensitive financial information during online transactions. This reassures customers that their payment details are safe and reduces the risk of fraudulent activities. Prioritizing secure digital payments helps the company establish itself as a trustworthy and reliable business.

Incorporating robust cybersecurity measures and offering secure digital payment options strengthens security and builds customer trust. These measures protect sensitive data and demonstrate the company's commitment to providing a safe and reliable online experience. This enhances customer trust and confidence in the company's ability to safeguard their information, fostering long-term relationships and loyalty.

8. Continuous Learning and Adaptability

Online Learning Platforms: Small and medium-sized businesses (SMBs) can access numerous online courses and resources. These resources allow SMBs to continuously upgrade their skills and knowledge, ensuring they remain relevant in a rapidly changing business landscape.

Conclusion

The dynamic relationship between SMBs and technology generates a wide range of opportunities. Technology is no longer an optional addition but an essential component of an SMB's strategy to succeed in today's business landscape. By leveraging the potential of digital tools and platforms, SMBs are surviving and positioning themselves as leaders in innovation, growth, and customer engagement in the digital era.

UNDERSTANDING TODAY'S DIGITAL LANDSCAPE

Overview of significant tech trends

The dawn of the 21st century has seen unprecedented technological advancements. These innovations have redefined industries, economies, and even our daily lives. This chapter provides a comprehensive overview of significant emerging tech trends, offering insights into their implications and potential trajectories.

1. Artificial Intelligence (AI) and Machine Learning (ML)

Overview: AI and ML refer to machines programmed to mimic human intelligence. They learn from data, make decisions, and improve over time.

Implications: AI has vast potential across sectors, from chatbots providing customer service to algorithms predicting market trends.

AI and ML significantly impact the business world, revolutionizing various operations and decision-making processes. Here are some ways in which AI and ML are changing the business landscape:

1. **Automation**: AI and ML technologies enable the automation of repetitive and mundane tasks, freeing employees to focus on more strategic and creative work. This increases productivity and efficiency.

2. **Data Analysis**: AI and ML algorithms can quickly and accurately analyze vast amounts of data, extracting valuable insights and patterns humans may miss. This helps in making data-driven decisions and identifying new business opportunities.

3. **Personalization**: AI and ML algorithms can analyze customer data and behavior to deliver personalized experiences and recommendations. This enhances customer satisfaction and drives customer loyalty.

4. **Predictive Analytics**: By analyzing historical data, AI and ML algorithms can make predictions and forecasts, helping businesses anticipate trends, identify risks, and optimize operations.

5. **Customer Service**: AI-powered chatbots and virtual assistants can provide instant and personalized customer support, improving response times and customer satisfaction.

6. **Fraud Detection**: AI and ML algorithms can detect patterns and anomalies in data, enabling businesses to identify and prevent fraudulent activities.

7. **Supply Chain Optimization**: AI and ML can optimize supply chain operations by predicting demand, optimizing inventory levels, and improving logistics and delivery processes.

8. **Marketing and Advertising**: AI and ML can analyze customer preferences and behavior to create targeted marketing campaigns, optimize ad placements, and personalize content, leading to more effective marketing strategies.

Overall, AI and ML technologies are transforming how businesses operate, allowing for increased efficiency, improved decision-making, enhanced customer experiences, and the ability to stay ahead in today's competitive market.

2. Internet of Things (IoT)

Overview: IoT involves connecting everyday objects to the internet, allowing them to collect and exchange data.

Implications: The Internet of Things (IoT) promises a future where everything is integrated and optimized for user convenience and efficiency. Its applications range from smart homes to connected healthcare.

The Internet of Things (IoT) is revolutionizing the business world in several ways:

1. **Operational Efficiency**: IoT allows businesses to collect real-time data from interconnected devices and sensors, enabling them to monitor and optimize operational processes like inventory management, supply chain logistics, and equipment maintenance. By automating and streamlining these processes, businesses can improve efficiency, reduce costs, and minimize downtime.

2. **Data-Driven Decision Making**: With IoT, businesses can gather large amounts of data from diverse sources. This data provides valuable insights into customer behavior, product performance, and market trends. Companies can make more informed decisions by analyzing this data, identifying improvement opportunities, and developing targeted strategies to meet customer needs.

3. **Improved Customer Experiences**: IoT enables businesses to create personalized and customized customer experiences. Companies can deliver tailored products and services by collecting and analyzing data on customer preferences, behavior, and usage patterns. For example, smart home devices

can learn individual preferences and adjust settings accordingly, providing a personalized and convenient living experience.

4. **New Business Models**: IoT opens up opportunities for new business models and revenue streams. For instance, businesses can offer IoT-enabled products as a service, providing ongoing maintenance and updates. Additionally, IoT data can be monetized by providing valuable insights to third parties or selling aggregated data to analytics companies.

5. **Supply Chain Optimization**: IoT allows businesses to track and monitor goods throughout the supply chain in real-time. This visibility enables better inventory management, improved demand forecasting, and optimized logistics. By streamlining the supply chain, businesses can reduce costs, minimize waste, and improve efficiency.

6. **Enhanced Safety and Security**: IoT technologies improve safety and security in various industries. For example, IoT sensors in manufacturing can detect potential hazards and automatically shut down equipment to prevent accidents. In cybersecurity, IoT devices can have robust security measures to protect sensitive data and prevent unauthorized access.

IoT transforms the business world by enabling excellent connectivity, data-driven insights, operational efficiency, and enhanced customer experiences. Embracing IoT technologies and leveraging interconnected devices can give businesses a competitive edge and drive innovation in today's digital era.

3. Augmented Reality (AR) and Virtual Reality (VR)

Overview: While virtual reality (VR) immerses users in a wholly digital environment, augmented reality (AR) overlays digital content in the real world.

Implications: Beyond gaming, these technologies are revolutionizing industries such as education (virtual classrooms), real estate (virtual property tours), and healthcare (virtual surgeries).

AR and VR technologies are revolutionizing the business world by transforming various industries and enhancing customer experiences. Here are some ways in which AR and VR are changing the business landscape:

1. **Product Visualization**: AR and VR allow businesses to showcase their products or services in immersive and interactive ways. Customers can visualize and experience effects before purchasing, leading to increased engagement and higher conversion rates. For example, furniture companies can use AR to enable customers to virtually place and see how furniture would look in their homes.

2. **Training and Education**: AR and VR provide realistic and immersive training experiences, enabling employees to learn and practice complex tasks in a safe and controlled environment. This is particularly beneficial in healthcare, manufacturing, and aviation industries. VR simulations can replicate real-life scenarios, improving learning outcomes and reducing training costs.

3. **Virtual Meetings and Collaboration**: AR and VR technologies enable remote teams to collaborate effectively by simulating face-to-face interactions. Virtual meeting spaces and avatars can make remote communication more engaging and productive. Businesses can save time and resources by reducing the need for travel while fostering collaboration across different locations.

4. **Virtual Tours and Real Estate**: AR and VR allow businesses in the real estate industry to provide virtual property tours, giving potential buyers a realistic sense of space and design. This saves time for both buyers and sellers and expands the reach of property listings. Architects and designers can also use AR and VR to showcase their designs to clients, enhancing communication and visualization.

5. **Marketing and Advertising**: AR and VR technologies offer innovative ways to engage customers with interactive and immersive marketing campaigns. Businesses can create virtual experiences or games to promote products or services, increasing brand awareness and customer engagement. For example, retailers can use AR to allow customers to try on virtual clothes or accessories.

6. **Data Visualization**: AR and VR can be used to visualize complex data sets more intuitively and immersively. Businesses can explore data in 3D space, enabling better understanding and analysis. This can be particularly useful in architecture, data analytics, and scientific research.

7. **Enhanced Customer Experiences**: AR and VR technologies enable businesses to provide unique and personalized customer experiences. Whether through AR-powered apps, immersive VR environments, or interactive virtual showrooms, businesses can create memorable and engaging experiences that differentiate them from competitors.

Overall, AR and VR technologies revolutionize how businesses engage with customers, train employees, market products, and collaborate across distances. By leveraging these technologies, companies can enhance customer experiences, improve operational efficiency, and gain a competitive edge in today's increasingly digital world.

4. Blockchain and Cryptocurrency

Overview: Blockchain is a decentralized ledger of transactions, with cryptocurrency being its most famous application.

Implications: Blockchain can potentially revolutionize sectors that require secure and transparent transactions, such as banking, supply chain, and voting systems.

Blockchain technology and cryptocurrency are revolutionizing the business world in several ways:

1. **Secure and Transparent Transactions**: Blockchain provides a decentralized and transparent ledger of transactions, eliminating the need for intermediaries. This enhances transaction security and efficiency. Businesses can use blockchain to securely record and verify transactions, reducing fraud and ensuring data integrity.
2. **Streamlined Supply Chain Management**: Blockchain improves supply chain management by creating an immutable record of every transaction and movement of goods. This enables real-time tracking and tracing of products, ensuring transparency and authenticity. Blockchain also facilitates efficient and secure information sharing among supply chain stakeholders.
3. **Efficient Cross-Border Payments**: Cryptocurrencies powered by blockchain technology enable fast and cost-effective cross-border payments. Traditional payment systems often need to be faster and involve high fees. Cryptocurrencies streamline international transactions, eliminating intermediaries and reducing costs.

4. **Crowdfunding and Fundraising**: Cryptocurrencies have led to the rise of Initial Coin Offerings (ICOs), allowing businesses to raise funds by issuing digital tokens. ICOs provide an alternative to traditional fundraising methods, offering a global pool of investors and reducing barriers to entry.

5. **Smart Contracts**: Smart contracts are self-executing agreements coded on blockchain platforms. They automatically execute predefined conditions without intermediaries. Intelligent contracts streamline business processes, reduce costs, and increase efficiency by automating contract management, payments, and other transactions.

6. **Improved Data Security**: Blockchain technology uses cryptographic algorithms to enhance data security, protecting sensitive business information from unauthorized access and breaches. By leveraging blockchain, businesses can enhance data privacy and build customer trust.

7. **Digital Identity Verification**: Blockchain enables secure and tamper-proof digital identity verification, crucial in finance, healthcare, and e-commerce. Blockchain-based identity solutions streamline customer onboarding, reduce fraud, and enhance data protection.

8. **Tokenization of Assets**: Blockchain allows for the digital representation and trading of physical and digital assets. This provides liquidity and fractional ownership. Businesses can tokenize assets like real estate, artwork, or intellectual property, opening up new investment opportunities and enabling efficient asset management.

9. **Decentralized Applications (DApps)**: Blockchain platforms enable the development of decentralized applications built on the blockchain. These applications offer transparent, secure, and user-centric business models and services. DApps disrupt

industries by removing intermediaries and enabling direct peer-to-peer interactions.

10. **Data Monetization and Ownership**: Blockchain technology gives individuals more control over their data and the ability to decide how it is shared and monetized. Businesses can create data marketplaces on blockchain, where individuals can securely sell their data. This allows individuals to monetize their data while maintaining control and privacy.

Blockchain technology and cryptocurrency are transforming the business world by providing secure and transparent transactions, streamlining processes, improving data security, enabling new fundraising methods, and revolutionizing how businesses operate and interact with customers.

5. 5G Connectivity

Overview: 5G, the fifth generation of mobile network technology, promises faster speeds, reduced latency, and improved connectivity.

Implications: Enhanced connectivity can facilitate smoother AR/VR experiences, real-time gaming, and instant data transfer between devices.

5G connectivity revolutionizes the business world by providing faster speeds, reduced latency, and improved connectivity. Here are some ways in which 5G is changing the business landscape:

1. **Enhanced Mobile Experiences**: With 5G, businesses can deliver their customers more prosperous and immersive mobile experiences. The increased bandwidth and lower latency enable seamless streaming of high-quality videos, augmented reality

(AR) and virtual reality (VR) experiences, and real-time interactive applications. This opens new business opportunities to engage with customers and provide innovative services.

2. **Internet of Things (IoT) Advancements**: 5G connectivity facilitates the growth of the Internet of Things (IoT) by supporting many connected devices. The higher capacity and lower latency of 5G networks enable real-time data transmission and faster response times for IoT applications. This allows businesses to optimize operations, improve efficiency, and create new IoT-enabled products and services.

3. **Industry 4.0 and Smart Manufacturing**: 5G enables smart manufacturing and Industry 4.0 initiatives. With its high-speed, low-latency connectivity, 5G allows real-time monitoring and control of manufacturing processes, remote maintenance and diagnostics, and seamless integration of robots and automation systems. This leads to increased productivity, reduced downtime, and improved operational efficiency.

4. **Remote Work and Collaboration**: 5G connectivity empowers remote work and collaboration by providing reliable, high-speed internet access. With 5G, businesses can facilitate seamless video conferencing, file sharing, and real-time collaboration on cloud-based platforms. This enables teams to work together more efficiently, regardless of their physical locations.

5. **Smart Cities and Infrastructure**: 5G connectivity is a crucial enabler of smart cities and infrastructure. The ultra-fast speeds and low latency of 5G networks support various smart applications, such as innovative traffic management, intelligent transportation systems, and connected infrastructure. This leads to improved efficiency, reduced congestion, and enhanced sustainability in urban environments.

6. **Real-Time Data Analytics**: 5G enables businesses to gather and analyze real-time data from various sources. This allows for faster and more accurate data analytics, leading to better decision-making and the ability to respond quickly to changing market conditions. Real-time insights from 5G-powered analytics can help businesses identify trends, optimize operations, and deliver personalized services.

7. **Emerging Technologies**: 5G acts as a catalyst for adopting and advancing emerging technologies. It provides the high-speed and low-latency connectivity required for technologies like autonomous vehicles, drones, remote surgeries, and smart homes. These technologies have the potential to disrupt industries and create new business opportunities.

5G connectivity transforms the business world by enabling faster and more reliable communication, driving innovation, and unlocking new possibilities across various industries. Businesses that leverage the power of 5G can gain a competitive edge, improve operational efficiency, and deliver enhanced customer experiences.

6. Quantum Computing

Overview: Quantum computers utilize the principles of quantum mechanics to process large amounts of data simultaneously.

Implications: Quantum computing has the potential to surpass significantly current computational speeds, leading to revolutionary advancements in areas such as cryptography, optimization problems, and complex system simulations.

Quantum computing is set to revolutionize the business world by providing unparalleled computational power and solving complex problems faster than traditional computers. Here are some ways in which quantum computing is transforming the business landscape:

1. **Advanced Data Analysis**: Quantum computers have the potential to analyze vast amounts of data and uncover intricate patterns and correlations that are beyond the capabilities of classical computers. This enables businesses to gain deeper insights into customer behavior, market trends, and complex datasets, leading to more informed decision-making and discovering hidden opportunities.

2. **Optimization and Efficiency**: Quantum computing can solve optimization problems critical to businesses across various industries. From supply chain optimization to logistics planning, quantum algorithms can find the most efficient solutions, reducing costs and improving operational efficiency. This has significant implications for transportation, finance, and manufacturing industries.

3. **Secure Communications and Cryptography**: Quantum computing also has the potential to strengthen cybersecurity. Quantum-resistant cryptographic algorithms can be developed to secure sensitive data and communications from future quantum attacks. Additionally, quantum communication protocols can provide unbreakable encryption, ensuring the confidentiality and integrity of business communications.

4. **Drug Discovery and Material Science**: Quantum computing can expedite the process of drug discovery and development by simulating complex molecular interactions and predicting drug efficacy. It can also advance material science by modeling and designing new materials with desired properties. These applications have the potential to revolutionize the pharmaceutical and materials industries.

5. **Financial Modeling and Risk Analysis**: Quantum computing can enhance financial modeling and risk analysis by simulating complex economic scenarios and analyzing investment portfolios. This enables businesses to make more accurate predictions and mitigate risks, improving financial decision-making and portfolio management.

6. **Machine Learning and Artificial Intelligence**: Quantum computing can enhance machine learning algorithms, enabling businesses to train more sophisticated models and make better predictions. Quantum machine learning algorithms can process more extensive datasets and uncover deeper insights, opening up new possibilities for AI applications in personalized marketing, fraud detection, and predictive analytics.

While quantum computing is still in its early stages of development, businesses are already exploring its potential applications. Quantum computing is expected to revolutionize industries, reshape business strategies, and unlock new opportunities for innovation and growth.

7. Edge Computing

Overview: Instead of relying on centralized data centers, edge computing processes data closer to where it is generated, such as on a local computer or IoT device.

Implications: This can result in faster data processing, decreased latency, and improved resource utilization.

Edge computing is transforming the business world by revolutionizing data processing and storage. Here are some ways in which edge computing is changing the business landscape:

1. **Faster Data Processing**: By processing data closer to the source, edge computing minimizes the need for data to travel to centralized data centers. This reduces latency and enables real-time data processing, allowing businesses to make faster decisions and respond rapidly to changing conditions. Industries such as autonomous vehicles, industrial automation, and remote monitoring greatly benefit from low-latency data processing provided by edge computing.

2. **Improved Reliability**: Edge computing enhances the reliability of business operations by reducing dependence on a centralized infrastructure. With edge devices processing data locally, businesses are less vulnerable to network outages or disruptions. Critical applications, such as healthcare monitoring systems or industrial control systems, can continue to function even if the connection to the cloud is temporarily lost.

3. **Bandwidth Optimization**: Businesses can optimize bandwidth usage by processing and filtering data at the edge. Only relevant and meaningful data is transmitted to the cloud, reducing the amount of data that needs to be transferred and stored. This saves on network costs and reduces the burden on centralized data centers.

4. **Real-Time Insights**: Edge computing enables businesses to gain real-time insights from the vast amount of data generated by IoT devices. For example, in smart cities, edge devices can process data from sensors in real time, allowing for immediate response to changing conditions, such as adjusting traffic signals based on current traffic patterns. Real-time insights empower businesses to make data-driven decisions and improve operational efficiency.

5. **Data Privacy and Security**: Edge computing addresses privacy and security concerns by keeping sensitive data closer to its source. Instead of transmitting sensitive data to the cloud, where it may be vulnerable to cyber threats, edge devices can process and store data locally, providing an additional layer of security. This is particularly important in healthcare, finance, and manufacturing industries, where data privacy and security are paramount.

6. **Offline Capabilities**: Edge computing allows businesses to operate offline or in low-connectivity environments. Edge devices can continue to process and store data locally, ensuring uninterrupted operations and data collection. This is especially beneficial for remote locations, mobile applications, or scenarios where internet connectivity is unreliable or limited.

7. **Scalability and Cost Efficiency**: Edge computing enables businesses to scale their operations and handle increasing amounts of data without overwhelming centralized data centers. Edge devices can distribute data processing and storage, reducing the need for expensive infrastructure upgrades. This scalability and cost efficiency make edge computing attractive for businesses looking to expand their IoT deployments or handle large-scale data processing.

8. **Real-Time Decision-Making**: With edge computing, businesses can make critical decisions in real time without relying on data to be transmitted to the cloud and back. This is particularly important in time-sensitive applications, such as industrial automation or autonomous vehicles, where immediate actions must be taken based on real-time data analysis.

Overall, edge computing revolutionizes the business world by enabling faster data processing, reducing latency, improving reliability, and enhancing data privacy and security. By leveraging edge computing, businesses can unlock new opportunities for real-time insights, optimize bandwidth usage, and ensure uninterrupted operations in today's increasingly connected and data-driven environment.

8. Robotics and Automation

Overview: Robotics involves the creation of machines that can move and function autonomously or semi-autonomously. Automation, on the other hand, focuses on systems that operate with minimal human intervention.

Implications: From manufacturing to healthcare, robotics and automation can enhance efficiency, decrease costs, and even accomplish tasks that surpass human capabilities.

Robotics and automation are transforming the business world by revolutionizing processes, enhancing efficiency, and enabling tasks that surpass human capabilities. Here are some ways in which robotics and automation are changing the business landscape:

1. **Increased Efficiency and Productivity**: Robotics and automation systems perform repetitive tasks precisely and quickly, enhancing efficiency and productivity. Automating manual and mundane tasks frees human resources for more strategic and value-added activities.
2. **Improved Safety**: Robots and automated systems perform hazardous tasks in environments that pose risks to human safety. This includes studies involving heavy lifting, exposure to harmful substances, or working in extreme conditions.

Deploying robots and automation improves workplace safety and reduces the risk of accidents and injuries.

3. **Cost Reduction**: Robotics and automation lead to long-term cost savings. Although the initial investment may be significant, automated systems operate continuously, require minimal maintenance, and reduce the need for human labor. This results in reduced operational costs, increased output, and improved profitability.

4. **Quality and Consistency**: Robots and automated systems consistently perform tasks accurately and precisely, improving product quality and consistency. This is particularly crucial in manufacturing and assembly processes, where even minor errors can have significant consequences. Automation ensures that products meet strict quality standards and customer expectations.

5. **Increased Flexibility and Scalability**: Robotics and automation allow businesses to adapt to changing demands and scale operations as needed. Automated systems can be reprogrammed or reconfigured to perform different tasks or accommodate varying production volumes. This agility allows businesses to respond quickly to market fluctuations and customer needs.

6. **Enhanced Customer Experiences**: Robotics and automation improve customer experiences by enabling faster and more efficient service delivery. For example, automated customer service systems handle inquiries and provide instant responses, reducing wait times and improving customer satisfaction. Robotic process automation (RPA) streamlines backend processes, ensuring smooth and seamless customer interactions.

7. **Advanced Analytics and Insights**: Robotics and automation generate vast amounts of data that can be analyzed for valuable insights. Businesses leverage data analytics and machine learning algorithms to optimize processes, identify improvement opportunities, and make data-driven decisions. This enables continuous optimization and innovation.

8. **Collaboration between Humans and Robots**: Collaborative robots, or cobots, enable humans and robots to work together in a shared workspace. Cobots assist human workers, enhance their capabilities, and perform tasks requiring human dexterity and robotic strength. This collaboration maximizes efficiency and productivity while ensuring a safe and ergonomic working environment.

9. **New Business Opportunities**: Robotics and automation create new business opportunities and disrupt traditional industries. For example, autonomous vehicles open up possibilities in transportation and logistics, while robots in healthcare and elderly care address the challenges of an aging population. Businesses embracing robotics and automation can explore new markets, deliver innovative products and services, and gain a competitive edge.

10. **Workforce Transformation**: Adopting robotics and automation requires businesses to adapt their workforce and develop new skill sets. While some jobs may be automated, new roles in robot programming, maintenance, and supervision emerge. Businesses must invest in upskilling and reskilling their workforce to ensure a smooth transition and leverage the benefits of robotics and automation.

Overall, robotics and automation revolutionize the business world by increasing efficiency, improving safety, reducing costs, enhancing customer experiences, and opening up new opportunities for innovation. By embracing these technologies, businesses can stay competitive, drive growth, and navigate the evolving digital landscape.

Conclusion

The tech trends discussed here provide a glimpse into a future influenced by innovation, integration, and digital transformation. Businesses, professionals, and everyday consumers must comprehend these trends. They are not only shaping industries but also reshaping the very fabric of society and human existence. Adaptability, continuous learning, and foresight become our most valuable assets as we navigate this ever-changing landscape.

The cost of ignoring the digital wave

The saying "adapt or perish" is particularly relevant in today's business environment. With digital transformation impacting various industries, companies that ignore or resist this change face a competitive disadvantage and put their very existence at risk. This chapter explores businesses' numerous costs when they disregard the digital revolution.

1. Lost Market Share

Diminished Visibility: In a world where consumers increasingly turn to the internet for their needs, not having a digital presence can make a business virtually invisible.

Reduced Competitiveness: Companies that utilize digital tools can provide better prices, convenience, and customer experiences. This can attract customers away from businesses that need to embrace these tools.

Case Study: The Traditional Indian Clothing Brand

One example of a brand that suffered significant market share loss due to its lack of digital presence and failure to utilize digital tools is a traditional Indian clothing brand with a long history.

Despite having a strong offline presence and a loyal customer base, the brand needed to recognize the growing importance of the digital wave. While competitors embraced e-commerce and social media platforms to reach a wider audience, this brand solely relied on brick-and-mortar stores.

As consumers increasingly turned to online shopping for convenience and variety, the brand's limited visibility severely impacted its market share. Potential customers, especially the younger generation, sought trendy fashion options and preferred the convenience of browsing and purchasing online. Without a digital presence, the brand failed to engage with these potential customers and lost out on a significant portion of the market.

Moreover, the brand's reluctance to embrace digital tools reduced competitiveness. Competitors utilize data analytics to effectively understand customer preferences and cater to their needs. They offered personalized recommendations, seamless shopping experiences, and competitive prices. In contrast, this traditional brand struggled to meet changing customer demands and deliver a comparable experience.

As a result of these shortcomings, the brand experienced a decline in sales and struggled to attract new customers. Despite its heritage and reputation, it ultimately lost significant market share to digitally-savvy competitors.

This case is a stark reminder that businesses must adapt and leverage digital platforms to stay competitive in today's digital age. Neglecting digital presence and tools can lead to a decline in market share, missed revenue opportunities, and an inability to meet evolving customer expectations.

2. Inefficiencies and Higher Operational Costs

Manual Processes: Without automation, businesses spend more time on repetitive tasks, which results in higher labor costs and an increased risk of errors.

Delayed Decision-Making: The lack of real-time data and digital analytics tools can hinder business decision-making, affecting responsiveness and adaptability.

Case Study: The Indian Retail Chain

An Indian retail chain with multiple stores across the country faced significant growth challenges due to inefficiencies and higher operational costs resulting from manual processes and delayed decision-making.

The chain heavily relied on manual inventory management, which involved time-consuming tasks such as manually counting stock, recording data on paper, and reconciling inventory records. This manual process consumed significant labor and introduced errors and inaccuracies. Consequently, the chain frequently experienced stockouts or excess inventory, leading to missed sales opportunities and increased costs.

Additionally, the absence of real-time data and digital analytics tools hindered the chain's ability to make informed and timely decisions. Managers had to rely on outdated reports and manual calculations to analyze sales data, identify trends, and forecast demand. This delayed decision-making process restricted the chain's agility and responsiveness to market changes, resulting in missed opportunities to optimize inventory levels, adjust pricing, and adapt marketing strategies.

The inefficiencies caused by manual processes and delayed decision-making led to higher operational costs for the retail chain. The labor-intensive nature of inventory management required a larger workforce, increasing labor expenses. Furthermore, the inability to optimize inventory levels and respond quickly to changing market demands resulted in excess inventory carrying costs and missed revenue opportunities.

As competition intensified and consumer expectations evolved, the retail chain needed help to keep up with more technologically advanced competitors. These competitors leveraged automation and real-time analytics to streamline operations, optimize inventory, and deliver a superior customer experience. In contrast, the manual processes and delayed decision-making of the Indian retail chain resulted in higher costs, reduced efficiency, and a diminished ability to meet customer demands.

Eventually, the chain recognized the need to embrace digital transformation to overcome these challenges. By implementing an integrated inventory management system and adopting data analytics tools, they could automate inventory tracking, optimize stock levels, and make data-driven decisions. This digital shift allowed the chain to improve operational efficiency, reduce costs, and enhance customer experience.

The case of the Indian retail chain highlights the detrimental impact of manual processes and delayed decision-making on business growth. By failing to adapt to digital tools and automation, the chain experienced inefficiencies, higher operational costs, and a loss of competitiveness. Embracing digital transformation became crucial to overcoming these challenges and ensuring future success.

3. Diminished Customer Experience

Limited Engagement: Without digital channels, businesses miss many opportunities to interact with customers, ranging from social media to mobile apps.

Reduced Personalization: Digital tools enable customized experiences based on customer preferences and behaviors. These tools should be considered to improve customer loyalty and satisfaction.

Case Study: The Indian Beauty Brand

An Indian beauty brand with a solid offline presence and a loyal customer base faced challenges in customer experience due to limited engagement and reduced personalization resulting from their lack of digital channels.

This brand has offered a wide range of beauty products for many years through physical stores. However, with the shift in consumer behavior towards online shopping and digital interactions, the brand needed to adapt and establish a robust digital presence.

The absence of digital channels meant missed opportunities for the brand to engage with customers. They could not utilize social media platforms to connect with their target audience, understand their preferences, and provide real-time updates on new products or promotions. This limited engagement made it difficult for the brand to stay top-of-mind with customers and create a sense of community around their products.

Furthermore, the brand's lack of digital tools prevented it from offering personalized experiences to its customers. Digital platforms enable businesses to gather data on customer preferences, purchase histories, and browsing behavior, which can be used for tailored recommendations and targeted marketing campaigns. Unfortunately, without access to these insights, the Indian beauty brand struggled to deliver personalized experiences that could enhance customer loyalty and satisfaction.

Consequently, the brand experienced a decline in customer engagement and loyalty. Competitors who embraced digital strategies could offer personalized product recommendations, virtual try-on experiences, and interactive customer support. These digital-savvy competitors created a seamless customer journey that catered to individual preferences and needs, putting the Indian beauty brand at a disadvantage.

The limited engagement and reduced personalization resulting from the brand's lack of digital channels significantly impacted its customer experience. Customers, particularly the younger generation, sought convenience, personalized recommendations, and interactive experiences. Without these digital capabilities, the Indian beauty brand struggled to meet customer expectations, leading to diminished customer satisfaction and a potential loss of market share.

This case serves as a reminder that businesses must prioritize digital engagement and personalization to deliver exceptional customer experiences. Neglecting these aspects can result in declining customer loyalty, missed revenue opportunities, and an inability to keep up with digitally-driven competitors.

4. Reduced Innovation Potential

Lagging: Businesses miss out on valuable insights and tools that can drive innovation in products, services, or processes if they do not leverage digital platforms.

Stagnation: Reluctance to embrace the digital wave can create a culture resistant to change, hindering creativity and forward-thinking.

Case Study: The Indian Electronics Manufacturer

An Indian electronics manufacturer with a long-standing reputation in the market experienced a decline in innovation potential due to its reluctance to embrace the digital wave. As the industry evolved with technological advancements, this brand failed to keep pace, resulting in stagnation and missed opportunities for innovation.

While competitors invested in digital transformation and explored emerging technologies, this Indian brand remained rooted in traditional manufacturing processes and outdated systems. The company relied on legacy machinery and manual workflows, which limited its ability to scale operations efficiently and adapt to changing market demands.

As a result, the brand needed to catch up in product innovation and needed help to introduce new features and functionalities that could meet evolving customer needs. Competitors, leveraging digital platforms and data analytics, were able to identify emerging trends, gather customer insights, and develop cutting-edge products. In contrast, this Indian brand was constrained by its resistance to change and reliance on outdated practices.

The reluctance to embrace digital tools and technologies created a culture of stagnation within the organization. Employees were hesitant to explore new ideas or challenge existing processes, as they needed more resources and support for innovation. This hindered the brand's ability to foster a culture of creativity and forward-thinking, further exacerbating its reduced innovation potential.

Consequently, the Indian electronics manufacturer struggled to keep up with competitors who introduced innovative products and captured market share. Incredibly tech-savvy customers were drawn to brands offering advanced features, intelligent capabilities, and seamless integration with digital ecosystems. The stagnant Indian brand failed to resonate with these customers and saw declining sales and market relevance.

This case is a cautionary tale for businesses that neglect innovation in the face of digital advancements. By lagging and resisting change, the Indian electronics manufacturer missed valuable opportunities to drive product innovation, meet customer expectations, and secure a competitive edge in the market.

It emphasizes the importance of embracing the digital wave and fostering a culture of innovation to stay relevant and thrive in an ever-changing business landscape.

5. Talent Drain

Attracting Top Talent: The new generation of workers is looking for technologically advanced and forward-thinking employers. Not embracing digital adoption can deter potential top-tier talent.

Training and Development: Digital platforms provide numerous opportunities for enhancing employee skills. Neglecting these platforms can result in a skills gap within the workforce.

Case Study: The Indian Tech Startup

An Indian tech startup in the IT services industry experienced a significant talent drain due to its failure to attract top talent and invest in training and development. Despite having ambitious goals and promising projects, this startup struggled to compete with more technologically advanced companies in the talent market.

The startup's reluctance to embrace digital tools and modern technologies hindered its ability to attract new workers seeking technologically advanced and forward-thinking employers. Consequently, top-tier talent often chose to join competitors that offered more growth opportunities, innovation, and exposure to cutting-edge technologies.

Furthermore, the lack of investment in training and development exacerbated the talent drain. While other companies provided comprehensive training programs and continuous skill development opportunities, this startup failed to prioritize employee growth and upskilling. As a result, employees felt that their career progression could have been more active, limiting their professional development and diminishing their enthusiasm for the company.

The talent drain severely impacted the startup's ability to deliver high-quality services and drive innovation. Without the necessary expertise and skills, the company struggled to acquire new clients and keep up with the rapidly changing technology landscape. Consequently, it lost market share to competitors who invested in attracting and retaining top talent.

This case is a cautionary tale for businesses that neglect the importance of attracting top talent and investing in training and development. By failing to adapt to the expectations of the new workforce and provide opportunities for growth and skill enhancement, the Indian tech startup experienced a significant talent drain, hindering its competitiveness and growth potential.

It underscores the importance of building a strong employer brand, offering continuous learning opportunities, and fostering a culture of innovation to attract and retain top talent in today's digital age.

6. Security Vulnerabilities

Outdated Systems: Legacy systems may need the latest security measures, making them vulnerable to breaches and cyberattacks.

Lack of Compliance: As regulations evolve, particularly in data protection, businesses require digital tools to ensure compliance and prevent possible legal consequences.

Case Study: The Indian Banking Firm

An Indian banking firm learned a harsh lesson about the risks associated with outdated systems and lack of compliance when it experienced security vulnerabilities that exposed customer data to potential breaches.

The banking firm had been operating for several decades and had built a reputation for reliability and trust. However, as technology advanced and cybersecurity threats became more sophisticated, the firm needed help maintaining security measures.

The firm's outdated systems, which relied on legacy infrastructure and software, needed the latest security patches and protocols. This made them vulnerable to cyberattacks that could exploit known vulnerabilities. Additionally, the firm had not implemented robust encryption methods or multi-factor authentication, increasing the risk of unauthorized access to sensitive customer data.

Unfortunately, the firm's lack of compliance with evolving data protection regulations exacerbated the security vulnerabilities. It had not implemented necessary measures to protect customer data by the latest privacy laws, exposing them to legal and financial consequences.

The consequences of these security vulnerabilities were severe. Cybercriminals successfully targeted the banking firm, gaining unauthorized access to customer records, including personal and financial information. This breach not only compromised the privacy and security of customers but also damaged the firm's reputation and eroded customer trust.

The fallout from the security breach was extensive. The banking firm faced legal actions and fines due to non-compliance with data protection regulations. Additionally, affected customers needed more confidence in the firm's ability to safeguard their information, leading to a significant loss of business and revenue.

This unfortunate incident serves as a reminder of the critical importance of prioritizing cybersecurity and compliance in today's digital landscape. Businesses, especially those dealing with sensitive customer data, must invest in robust security measures, regularly update their systems, and ensure compliance with relevant regulations. Failing to do so can result in security vulnerabilities, reputational damage, legal consequences, and substantial financial losses.

Organizations must stay vigilant, adopt best practices in cybersecurity, and prioritize compliance to protect their customers and their long-term viability in an increasingly digital world.

7. Missed Revenue Opportunities

Global Markets: E-commerce and digital platforms allow small and medium-sized businesses (SMBs) to reach international audiences. With digital adoption, SMBs would benefit from a potential revenue stream.

New Revenue Models: Digital transformation can reveal new sources of revenue, whether it's through online sales, digital products, or subscription models.

Case Study: The Indian Handicraft Brand

An Indian handicraft brand renowned for its exquisite traditional products missed significant revenue opportunities due to its failure to adapt to changes in global markets and new revenue models.

For many years, this brand flourished by serving a local customer base and exporting its handicrafts to a limited number of international markets. However, the emergence of e-commerce and digital platforms transformed the global marketplace, opening up new avenues for revenue generation.

While competitors embraced digital adoption and utilized online platforms to reach global audiences, this Indian brand hesitated and relied solely on its traditional distribution channels. As a result, it could have capitalized on the growing demand for conventional handicrafts from customers worldwide.

Furthermore, the brand's resistance to embracing new revenue models hindered its growth potential. It relied on a one-time purchase model, where customers would buy its products as souvenirs or decorative pieces. However, changing consumer behavior and preferences called for innovative revenue models such as subscription boxes, customization options, and online marketplaces.

Domestic and international competitors seized these emerging revenue models, offering a wide range of products and services that catered to evolving customer demands. They leveraged e-commerce platforms, social media marketing, and influencer collaborations to attract a global customer base and establish recurring revenue streams. In contrast, this Indian handicraft brand failed to adapt its business model and explore new revenue opportunities.

Consequently, the brand experienced a decline in sales and missed potential revenue growth from international markets and new revenue models. Customers worldwide turned to digitally enabled platforms to discover unique handicrafts and engage with brands that provided a seamless online shopping experience. Without a solid digital presence and a diversified revenue model, the Indian handicraft brand struggled to seize these opportunities and lost market share to digitally-savvy competitors.

This case is a stark reminder that businesses must adapt to changing global markets and explore new revenue models to thrive in the digital age. These opportunities must be considered to avoid missed revenue potential, declining market share, and an inability to meet evolving customer expectations. To avoid being left behind, brands must embrace digital transformation, leverage online platforms, and innovate their revenue models to unlock growth in the global marketplace.

8. Inability to Gauge Market Sentiment

Feedback Loop: Digital platforms provide real-time feedback, whether through reviews, comments, or social media. These are necessary for businesses to be aware of market sentiments, needs, or grievances.

Case Study: The Indian Mobile Phone Manufacturer

An Indian mobile phone manufacturer is an example of a brand that failed to understand market sentiment and faced severe consequences.

Initially, this brand gained prominence in the Indian mobile phone market by offering affordable smartphones. However, the brand needed to adapt as the market evolved and customer preferences changed.

While competitors embraced technological advancements, improved features, and appealing designs, this Indian brand remained stagnant. It continued to release smartphones with outdated specifications, limited features, and uninspiring designs, failing to meet the evolving customer demands.

In contrast, competitors launched smartphones with innovative features, sleek designs, and competitive pricing. They utilized market research, customer feedback, and social media listening to understand market sentiment and develop products that resonated with consumers.

Consequently, the Indian brand experienced a decline in sales and market share. Customers flocked to competitors' smartphones that offered superior performance, advanced features, and a better overall user experience. The brand's failure to understand market sentiment and adapt to changing customer needs resulted in missed revenue opportunities and a loss of market relevance.

This case serves as a reminder that businesses must actively listen to their customers, monitor market trends, and adjust their offerings accordingly. Refrain from understanding market sentiment to avoid a significant loss of market share, damage to brand reputation, and an inability to compete in a rapidly evolving industry.

To remain competitive, brands must embrace customer feedback, leverage data analytics and market research, and continuously innovate their products and services based on market sentiment. Doing so can ensure their offerings align with customer expectations and stay ahead of the curve in a dynamic marketplace.

Conclusion

The digital wave is not just another trend; it is the foundation of the modern business ecosystem. Ignoring it does not mean maintaining the status quo; it is a step backward. For businesses to succeed, it is not optional to understand, adapt to, and harness the digital revolution—it is imperative. The consequences of neglecting this wave are varied and often irreversible. Embracing the digital age is about staying relevant, ensuring survival, and fostering growth in a rapidly evolving world.

THE BASICS: MUST-HAVE TECHNOLOGIES FOR EVERY SMB

The role of a robust website

In today's digital ecosystem, a company's website is not just an accessory but a central pillar of its identity, operations, and outreach. Serving as the digital storefront and often the initial point of interaction with potential customers, the significance of a robust website cannot be emphasized enough. This chapter will delve into the various roles that an entire website plays in the modern business landscape.

1. Establishing Brand Identity

Digital Handshake: Just like first impressions matter in personal interactions, a website allows businesses to create a lasting impression on visitors.

Brand Consistency: A website with consistent design, logos, and content reinforces brand identity and creates a memorable image in the consumer's mind.

To establish a strong brand identity through their website, an Indian SMB can focus on the following strategies:

1. **Visual Branding:** Use consistent visual elements such as logos, colors, and typography that reflect the brand's personality and values. Incorporate Indian cultural elements or design motifs to create a unique and recognizable visual identity.

2. **Compelling Storytelling**: Share the story of the business, including its origins, mission, and values. Highlight any unique aspects of being an Indian SMB, such as local craftsmanship, sustainable practices, or community involvement. Connect with the audience emotionally through authentic storytelling.

3. **Localized Content**: Tailor the website content to resonate with the Indian audience. Use language, phrases, and cultural references familiar to the target market. Showcase how the SMB caters to the specific needs and preferences of Indian customers.

4. **Showcase Indian Heritage**: Highlight the rich cultural heritage of India through imagery, videos, or blog content. Showcase traditional practices, craftsmanship, or regional influences integral to the business. This can help create a sense of pride and connection among Indian customers.

5. **Customer Testimonials**: Feature testimonials and success stories from Indian customers to establish credibility and trust. Indian customers are more likely to trust a brand when they see positive feedback from their fellow citizens.

6. **Engage on Social Media**: Utilize popular social media platforms in India to engage with the target audience. Share relevant content, respond to comments and messages promptly, and participate in conversations to build a solid online presence and foster a sense of community.

7. **Local Partnerships**: Collaborate with other Indian SMBs, influencers, or organizations that align with the brand's values and target audience. This can help expand reach, gain credibility, and enhance brand visibility within the Indian market.

Remember, building a solid brand identity is an ongoing process. Regularly update the website with fresh content, engage with the audience through blogs or newsletters, and continuously seek feedback to refine and strengthen the brand's online presence.

By implementing these strategies, an Indian SMB can establish a strong brand identity through their website, connect with their target audience, build trust, and differentiate themselves in the competitive market.

2. Engaging and Informing Customers

Interactive Platform: Modern websites go beyond providing static information. They engage visitors by incorporating multimedia content, interactive features, and user-friendly interfaces.

Information Hub: A website offers users easy access to a wide range of information, including products and services, company history, and values.

To engage customers on their website, an Indian SMB can focus on the following strategies:

1. **Interactive Features**: Incorporate interactive elements on the website to make it engaging and user-friendly. This can include features like quizzes, polls, games, or interactive product demonstrations.
2. **Personalization**: Customize the website experience for each user based on their preferences, interests, or past interactions. This can be done by offering personalized product recommendations, targeted content, or offers.
3. **Live Chat or AI Chatbots**: Implement live chat or AI chatbot features to provide instant assistance and support to website visitors. This allows customers to ask questions, get real-time

responses, and receive personalized recommendations or guidance.

4. **User-Generated Content**: Encourage customers to share their experiences, reviews, or testimonials on the website. This engages customers and builds social proof and trust among potential customers.

5. **Responsive Design**: Ensure that the website is optimized for mobile devices, as many Indian internet users access websites through their smartphones. A responsive design provides a seamless and user-friendly experience across different devices.

6. **Social Media Integration**: Integrate social media platforms into the website to allow customers to share content, products, or reviews easily. This helps expand the business's reach and encourages customer engagement and interaction.

7. **Gamification**: Implement gamification elements on the website to make the customer experience more enjoyable and interactive. This can include reward systems, challenges, or competitions incentivizing customer participation and engagement.

8. **Regular Updates and Fresh Content**: Keep the website updated with fresh and relevant content, such as blogs, articles, or videos. This encourages customers to revisit the website and stay engaged with the brand.

By implementing these strategies, an Indian SMB can create an engaging and interactive website that effectively captures and retains customers' attention, fostering a strong connection and driving customer loyalty.

3. Building Credibility and Trust

Professionalism: A well-designed and functional website conveys professionalism, increasing the likelihood of visitors trusting and engaging with the business.

Testimonials and Reviews: Showcasing customer feedback and success stories can strengthen a company's reputation and build trust among potential clients.

To build credibility and trust on their website, an Indian SMB can focus on the following strategies:

1. **Professional Design**: A well-designed website conveys professionalism and attention to detail. It is essential to have a visually appealing and user-friendly interface that reflects the brand's identity and values.
2. **Testimonials and Reviews**: Positive customer feedback and success stories on the website can strengthen the company's reputation and build trust among potential clients. Indian SMBs can gather testimonials from satisfied customers and prominently display them on their websites.
3. **Case Studies and Use Cases**: Highlighting case studies and real-life examples of how the business has helped its customers can demonstrate the credibility and effectiveness of its products or services. Indian SMBs can showcase specific use cases that resonate with their target audience and prove the value they provide.
4. **Trust Badges and Certifications**: Displaying trust badges and certifications relevant to the industry or niche can instill confidence in visitors. Indian SMBs can obtain certifications or

affiliations from reputable organizations to enhance credibility and trustworthiness.

5. **Secure Payment Options**: If the Indian SMB offers e-commerce capabilities on their website, ensuring secure payment options and prominently displaying security badges can reassure customers about their personal and financial information safety.

6. **Transparent Policies**: Being transparent about policies, such as return and refund policies, shipping information, and privacy policies, builds trust with customers. Indian SMBs should communicate these policies on their website to demonstrate their commitment to customer satisfaction.

7. **Customer Support**: Providing accessible and responsive customer support channels, such as live chat, email, or phone, can give customers confidence that their concerns will be addressed promptly. Indian SMBs should display contact information and set clear expectations for response times.

8. **Social Proof**: Leveraging social proof, such as displaying the number of customers served, positive customer reviews, or testimonials from well-known individuals or organizations, can enhance credibility. Indian SMBs can encourage customers to leave reviews or share their experiences on social media platforms.

9. **Consistency and Reliability**: Consistently delivering on promises and ensuring reliable product or service quality builds trust over time. Indian SMBs should focus on providing a consistent and reliable experience to establish a reputation for dependability.

By implementing these strategies, an Indian SMB can establish credibility and trust on its website, reassuring potential customers and encouraging them to engage with the business.

4. Driving Sales and Conversions

E-commerce Capabilities: A website serves as a 24/7 storefront for businesses selling products or services, catering to customers worldwide.

Lead Generation: Websites can assist businesses in capturing leads and expanding their customer base through contact forms, newsletter sign-ups, and other engagement tools.

To drive sales and conversions on their website, an Indian SMB can focus on the following strategies:

1. **E-commerce Capabilities**: Implementing e-commerce capabilities on the website allows the business to sell products or services online, catering to customers worldwide. This provides convenience and accessibility, enabling customers to purchase anytime.
2. **Lead Generation**: Utilize contact forms, newsletter sign-ups, and other engagement tools to capture leads and expand the customer base. Encourage visitors to provide their contact information in exchange for exclusive offers, discounts, or valuable content.
3. **Compelling Product Descriptions**: Create persuasive and detailed product descriptions highlighting the offerings' unique selling points and benefits. Use high-quality images or videos to showcase the products from different angles and provide a clear understanding of what customers can expect.

4. **Clear Call-to-Action**: Place clear and prominent call-to-action buttons or links throughout the website, guiding visitors toward purchasing or taking the desired action. Use action-oriented language and create a sense of urgency to encourage conversions.

5. **Customer Reviews and Testimonials**: To build trust and credibility, display positive customer reviews and testimonials. Indian customers are more likely to purchase when they see feedback from fellow customers who have had a positive experience with the brand.

6. **Discounts and Promotions**: Offer exclusive discounts, promotions, or bundle deals to incentivize customers to purchase. Limited-time offers or special discounts for Indian festivals or occasions can create a sense of urgency and drive conversions.

7. **Cross-Selling and Upselling**: Recommend related products or suggest upgrades to customers during purchasing. This can increase the average order value and encourage customers to explore additional offerings.

8. **Abandoned Cart Recovery**: Implement strategies to recover abandoned carts by sending follow-up emails or offering incentives to encourage customers to complete their purchases. This can include personalized discount codes or reminders of the items left in the cart.

9. **Responsive and User-Friendly Design**: Ensure that the website is optimized for mobile devices, as many Indian internet users access websites through smartphones. A responsive design provides a seamless and user-friendly experience, increasing the likelihood of conversions.

10. **Secure Payment Options**: Offer fast, convenient payment options to instill customer confidence. Display trust badges or

security certifications to reassure customers about the safety of their personal and financial information.

11. **Social Proof and Influencer Collaborations**: Leverage social proof by featuring endorsements or collaborations with influencers or well-known individuals in the industry. This can enhance credibility and encourage conversions.

12. **Remarketing and Retargeting**: Utilize remarketing and retargeting strategies to reach out to website visitors who have shown interest but have yet to convert. Display targeted ads or send personalized emails to remind them about the products they viewed or abandoned in their cart.

By implementing these strategies, an Indian SMB can effectively drive sales and conversions on its website, maximizing its potential as a revenue-generating platform.

5. Enhancing Customer Support

FAQs and Chatbots: Many websites have FAQ sections or AI-driven chatbots that answer common customer queries instantly.

Support Portals: Websites can host ticket systems, support forums, or live chat options, offering efficient customer service channels.

To enhance customer support through their website, an Indian SMB can focus on the following strategies:

1. **FAQs and Chatbots**: Implement a Frequently Asked Questions (FAQ) section on the website to address common customer queries. Additionally, integrate AI-driven chatbots that can provide instant responses to customer inquiries. This ensures

that customers can find answers to their questions quickly and efficiently.

2. **Support Portals**: Create support portals on the website where customers can submit tickets or access live chat options for personalized assistance. This allows customers to reach out for help quickly and ensures that their concerns are addressed promptly.

3. **Knowledge Base**: Develop a comprehensive knowledge base that contains detailed information about products or services, troubleshooting guides, and step-by-step tutorials. This self-service resource empowers customers to find solutions to their problems independently, reducing the need for direct support.

4. **Feedback and Contact Forms**: Customers can quickly provide feedback or contact the business through dedicated forms on the website. Encourage customers to share their experiences, report issues, or ask questions. This helps gather valuable insights and enables the business to improve customer support based on customer feedback.

5. **Responsive and Timely Communication**: Ensure customer inquiries and messages are responded to promptly. Implement systems to track and manage customer communications efficiently. This includes acknowledging receipt of customer inquiries, providing regular updates, and resolving issues promptly.

6. **Personalization**: Utilize customer data to personalize the support experience. For returning customers, consider integrating customer support systems with customer relationship management (CRM) software to access their purchase history and previous interactions. This allows support representatives to provide tailored assistance based on customer needs and preferences.

7. **Social Media Integration**: Integrate social media platforms into the website's support channels. This enables customers to reach out for support or share their experiences through social media. Monitor social media platforms for customer inquiries or complaints and respond promptly to maintain a positive brand image.

8. **Continuous Improvement**: Regularly analyze customer support metrics and feedback to identify areas for improvement. Use customer satisfaction surveys, post-interaction feedback, and analytics to gain insights into the effectiveness of the support provided. Actively address any recurring issues, identify training needs for support agents, and make necessary improvements to enhance the overall customer support experience.

By implementing these strategies, an Indian SMB can enhance customer support through its website, ensuring that customers receive timely assistance, find answers to their questions, and have a positive experience with the business.

6. Optimizing Marketing Efforts

Data Collection and Analytics: Integrated analytics tools enable businesses to gather insights on visitor behavior, aiding in the refinement of marketing strategies and enhancing user experience.

Content Marketing Platform: A website is a hub for blogs, videos, infographics, and other content. It helps drive organic traffic and positions the company as an industry thought leader.

To optimize marketing efforts on their website, an Indian SMB can leverage data collection and analytics and a content marketing platform. Here's how:

1. **Data Collection and Analytics**: Integrated analytics tools enable businesses to gather valuable insights on visitor behavior, user demographics, and engagement metrics. By collecting and analyzing this data, an Indian SMB can refine its marketing strategies and enhance the user experience. Here are some critical steps:
   - Set up website analytics: Implement a robust analytics solution like Google Analytics to track website performance and user behavior.
   - Define critical metrics: Identify the key performance indicators (KPIs) most relevant to the business, such as website traffic, conversion rates, bounce rates, and user engagement metrics.
   - Analyze user behavior: Use analytics data to understand how visitors navigate the website, which pages they spend the most time on, and where they drop off in the conversion funnel.
   - Identify trends and opportunities: Analyze data trends to uncover opportunities for optimization. For example, identify high-performing landing pages or pages with a high exit rate to focus on improving user experience.
   - A/B testing: Conduct A/B tests to compare different versions of web pages, CTAs, or marketing campaigns and determine which performs better regarding conversions and user engagement.

    o   Personalization: Utilize analytics insights to personalize the website experience for different user segments, offering tailored content and recommendations based on user preferences and behavior.

2. **Content Marketing Platform**: A website is a hub for content marketing efforts, allowing an Indian SMB to drive organic traffic, position itself as an industry thought leader, and engage with its target audience. Here are some strategies to optimize content marketing efforts:

    o   Blogging: Publish regular blog posts that provide valuable insights, industry news, or helpful tips for the SMB's products or services. Optimize blog content with relevant keywords to improve search engine visibility.

    o   Video content: Create engaging and informative videos to showcase products, provide tutorials, or share industry expertise. Host videos on the website and optimize them for search engines and social media platforms.

    o   Infographics and visual content: Develop visually appealing infographics, images, or slideshows that convey information in a concise and shareable format. Optimize visual content for search engines and social media platforms.

    o   Lead magnets and gated content: Create downloadable resources, such as e-books, whitepapers, or guides, and offer them as lead magnets in exchange for visitor contact information. This helps build a subscriber base for email marketing campaigns.

o Social media integration: Integrate social media sharing buttons on the website to encourage visitors to share content on their social networks. This amplifies the reach of the SMB's content and drives organic traffic.

o SEO optimization: Optimize website content, including landing pages, blog posts, and product descriptions, with relevant keywords to improve search engine rankings and increase organic traffic.

o Content promotion: Actively promote website content through social media channels, email newsletters, industry forums, or guest blogging on relevant platforms. This increases visibility and drives traffic back to the website.

o Content updates: Regularly update website content to keep it fresh and relevant. This provides value to visitors and signals to search engines that the website is active and up-to-date.

By leveraging data collection and analytics and a content marketing platform, an Indian SMB can gain valuable insights into its audience, optimize marketing strategies, drive organic traffic, and establish itself as an industry leader, leading to increased brand visibility, customer engagement, and business growth.

7. Facilitating Business Operations

Integrated Systems: Modern websites can integrate with CRM systems, inventory management tools, and other backend operations. This integration helps streamline various business processes.

Remote Work and Collaboration: Websites can host portals and platforms for businesses with distributed teams that facilitate seamless collaboration and workflow management.

To facilitate business operations on their website, an Indian SMB can utilize integrated systems and remote work and collaboration tools. Here's how:

1. **Integrated Systems**: Modern websites can integrate various business tools and systems to streamline operations. For example:
   - CRM Integration: Integrate the website with a Customer Relationship Management (CRM) system to manage customer data, track interactions, and streamline sales and marketing processes.
   - Inventory Management: Connect the website with an inventory management tool to automate inventory tracking, stock updates, and order fulfillment processes.
   - Payment Gateways: Integrate secure and reliable payment gateways to facilitate smooth and secure online transactions.
   - Analytics and Reporting: Utilize website analytics tools to gather data on website performance, user behavior, and sales metrics. This data can be used to make informed business decisions and optimize operations.

2. **Remote Work and Collaboration**: A website can serve as a platform for businesses with distributed teams to facilitate remote work and collaboration. Here are some ways an Indian SMB can leverage their website:

- o Online Communication: Utilize chat tools, video conferencing platforms, or project management software integrated into the website to enable remote teams to communicate effectively and collaborate on projects.
- o Document Sharing and Collaboration: Use cloud-based document storage and collaboration tools integrated into the website to enable remote teams to work on shared documents in real-time, ensuring seamless collaboration and version control.
- o Task and Project Management: Implement project management tools integrated into the website to assign tasks, track progress, and ensure efficient workflow management among remote team members.
- o Access Control and Security: Set up secure user authentication and access control systems on the website to ensure that only authorized team members can access sensitive information or perform specific tasks.

By leveraging integrated systems and remote work and collaboration tools, an Indian SMB can streamline business operations, improve efficiency, and enable seamless collaboration among team members, irrespective of their physical locations.

8. Enhancing SEO and Visibility

Search Engine Ranking: A well-optimized website improves rankings, ensuring the business appears prominently in relevant search results.

Mobile Optimization: With growing users accessing websites through mobile devices, a responsive website design ensures a consistent user experience and enhances search rankings.

To enhance SEO and website visibility, Indian SMBs can focus on search engine ranking and mobile optimization.

Search Engine Ranking: A well-optimized website improves rankings, ensuring the business appears prominently in relevant search results. Here are some strategies Indian SMBs can implement:

1. **Keyword Research**: Conduct thorough keyword research to identify relevant keywords and phrases that potential customers are likely to search for. Incorporate these keywords into the website's content, including headings, titles, meta descriptions, and body text.
2. **Quality Content Creation**: Create high-quality, informative, and engaging content that aligns with the target audience's interests and needs. Regularly update the website with fresh content, such as blog posts, articles, or videos, targeting relevant keywords and providing valuable information to visitors.
3. **On-Page Optimization**: Optimize on-page elements, such as meta tags, headings, URLs, and image alt tags, to include relevant keywords and provide clear content descriptions. Ensure the website's structure is logical and easy for search engines to crawl and understand.
4. **Link Building**: Build high-quality backlinks from reputable and relevant websites. This can be achieved through guest blogging, partnerships, or sharing content others naturally link to. Backlinks help establish the website's authority and credibility in the eyes of search engines.

5. **Local SEO**: If the Indian SMB serves a specific geographic area, optimize the website for local search by including location-specific keywords and creating a Google My Business listing. Encourage satisfied customers to leave reviews on platforms like Google Reviews or Yelp.

Mobile Optimization: With growing users accessing websites through mobile devices, a responsive website design ensures a consistent user experience and enhances search rankings. Here's how Indian SMBs can optimize their website for mobile:

1. **Responsive Design**: Implement a responsive design that automatically adjusts the website's layout and content based on the device's access. This ensures the website looks and functions well on mobile devices, providing a positive user experience.

2. **Mobile-Friendly Content**: Optimize content for mobile consumption using shorter paragraphs, bullet points, and concise headings. Ensure that font sizes are legible on smaller screens and avoid using elements that may cause usability issues on mobile devices, such as flash animation.

3. **Page Speed Optimization**: Improve website loading speed, as slower loading times can negatively impact mobile user experience and search rankings. Compress images, minify CSS and JavaScript files, and leverage browser caching to optimize page speed.

4. **Mobile-First Indexing**: Design and structure the website with mobile users in mind, as search engines increasingly prioritize mobile-first indexing. Ensure that the most essential content and functionality are easily accessible on mobile devices.

5. **Mobile-Friendly Navigation**: Simplify mobile users' navigation using a clear and intuitive menu structure.

Implement touch-friendly buttons and ensure that essential actions, such as making a purchase or contacting the business, are easily accessible on mobile devices.

By focusing on search engine ranking and mobile optimization, Indian SMBs can improve their website's visibility in search results, attract organic traffic, and provide a seamless user experience across devices. This, in turn, can lead to increased brand awareness, higher engagement, and potential business growth.

Conclusion

A robust website is not just a digital address but a dynamic platform that impacts various aspects of a business. It is pivotal in driving sales, building brand identity, engaging customers, and facilitating backend operations. As the digital age advances, investing in a strong, versatile, and user-centric website is beneficial and essential for businesses aiming for growth and longevity in a digitally driven market landscape.

Sure! Here is a walkthrough of how an Indian SMB can implement the strategies mentioned above:

1. **Establishing Credibility and Trust**
   - Create a visually appealing, user-friendly website design reflecting the brand's identity and values.
   - Communicate the company's mission, values, and unique selling points on the website.
   - Display customer testimonials, reviews, or case studies to showcase positive experiences and build trust.
   - Implement secure payment options and prominently display trust badges or security certifications.

- o Develop comprehensive and transparent policies such as return and refund policies, shipping information, and privacy policies.
- o Ensure the website is regularly updated with relevant, engaging content to demonstrate industry expertise and customer commitment.

2. **Driving Sales and Conversions**
   - o Implement e-commerce capabilities to enable online sales, including seamless product browsing, selection, and checkout processes.
   - o Utilize lead generation strategies such as contact forms, newsletter sign-ups, and exclusive offers to capture customer information and expand the customer base.
   - o Create compelling and persuasive product descriptions with high-quality images or videos highlighting the product's unique features and benefits.
   - o Place clear and prominent call-to-action buttons throughout the website to guide visitors toward purchasing.
   - o Display customer reviews and testimonials to build trust and encourage potential customers to convert.
   - o Offer discounts, promotions, or bundle deals to incentivize purchases and create a sense of urgency.
   - o Implement cross-selling and upselling strategies to encourage customers to explore additional offerings.
   - o Utilize abandoned cart recovery tactics such as follow-up emails or personalized incentives to recover lost sales.

3. **Enhancing Customer Support**
   - Create a dedicated FAQ section on the website to address common customer queries.
   - Implement AI-driven chatbots to provide instant responses to customer inquiries.
   - Develop a comprehensive knowledge base with troubleshooting guides and tutorials for self-service support.
   - Provide easily accessible contact forms, live chat options, or ticket submission portals for personalized assistance.
   - Encourage customers to provide feedback and actively address their concerns promptly.
   - Utilize social media integration to provide support and monitor customer inquiries or complaints.
   - Continuously improve customer support based on feedback and metrics, ensuring responsive and personalized communication.

4. **Optimizing Marketing Efforts**
   - Implement analytics tools to gather insights on user behavior, demographics, and engagement metrics.
   - Conduct keyword research and optimize website content with relevant keywords to improve search engine rankings.
   - Leverage content marketing by regularly creating and publishing valuable and engaging content, such as blog posts, videos, and infographics.

- o Promote website content through social media channels, email newsletters, and industry forums to drive organic traffic.
- o Utilize SEO optimization techniques, including meta tags, headings, and URL optimization, to improve search rankings.
- o Collect and analyze data to refine marketing strategies and personalize the user experience.
- o Utilize data-driven remarketing and retargeting strategies to re-engage website visitors and encourage conversions.

5. **Facilitating Business Operations**
   - o Integrate the website with CRM systems, inventory management tools, and other backend operations to streamline business processes.
   - o For remote work and collaboration, utilize online communication tools, project management software, and document-sharing platforms.
   - o Implement secure user authentication and access control systems to protect sensitive information.
   - o Ensure the website is responsive and optimized for mobile devices to accommodate the growing number of mobile internet users.
   - o Regularly update website content and functionality to stay relevant and provide a seamless user experience.

6. **Enhancing SEO and Visibility**
   - Conduct thorough keyword research and incorporate relevant keywords into website content.
   - Create high-quality and informative content that aligns with user interests and needs.
   - Optimize on-page elements and build high-quality backlinks to improve search engine rankings.
   - Implement a responsive design and optimize website speed for mobile devices.
   - Regularly monitor website analytics and make data-driven improvements to enhance SEO and visibility.

By implementing these strategies, an Indian SMB can create a robust website that drives sales, enhances customer support, optimizes marketing efforts, facilitates business operations, and improves overall visibility and brand reputation.

Sure! A case study illustrates how implementing the abovementioned strategies helped an Indian SMB achieve significant growth and success.

Case Study: XYZ Clothing Store

XYZ Clothing Store is an Indian SMB that sells trendy clothing for young adults. They recognized the importance of having a robust website to expand their customer base, increase sales, and establish their brand in the competitive fashion industry.

1. **Establishing Credibility and Trust**
   - XYZ Clothing Store revamped its website with a modern and visually appealing design that reflected its brand identity.

- o They prominently displayed their mission, values, and unique selling points on the homepage, creating a solid brand image.
- o XYZ Clothing Store built trust and credibility among potential customers by showcasing customer testimonials and positive reviews.
- o They implemented secure payment options and prominently displayed trust badges, assuring customers of the safety of their transactions.

2. **Driving Sales and Conversions**
    - o XYZ Clothing Store implemented a user-friendly e-commerce platform on their website, allowing customers to browse and purchase their products online easily.
    - o They optimized product descriptions with compelling and persuasive content, highlighting each item's unique features and benefits.
    - o Offering personalized recommendations and cross-selling options encouraged customers to explore additional products and increase their average order value.
    - o XYZ Clothing Store used targeted email marketing campaigns to promote their latest collections, exclusive offers, and limited-time discounts, creating a sense of urgency and driving conversions.
    - o They successfully implemented abandoned cart recovery strategies, such as automated follow-up emails

with personalized incentives, significantly increasing recovered sales.

3. **Enhancing Customer Support**
   - XYZ Clothing Store created a comprehensive FAQ section on its website, addressing common customer queries about shipping, returns, and sizing.
   - They integrated an AI-driven chatbot that provided instant responses and personalized customer assistance, improving response times and customer satisfaction.
   - By actively monitoring and responding to customer inquiries and feedback on social media, XYZ Clothing Store demonstrated its commitment to excellent customer support.
   - They continuously collected and analyzed customer feedback to identify areas for improvement and implemented necessary changes in their products, services, and support processes.

4. **Optimizing Marketing Efforts**
   - XYZ Clothing Store implemented analytics tools to gather insights on customer behavior, preferences, and engagement metrics.
   - They regularly published high-quality blog posts on their website, sharing fashion tips, styling ideas, and industry news to engage their target audience and position themselves as fashion experts.

- o By promoting their blog content through social media channels, email newsletters, and collaborations with fashion influencers, they significantly increased organic traffic to their website.
- o XYZ Clothing Store utilized SEO optimization techniques, including keyword optimization, meta tags, and URL structure, to improve its search engine rankings and visibility.
- o They leveraged data-driven remarketing campaigns to re-engage website visitors and encourage them to complete their purchases, increasing conversions and customer retention.

5. **Facilitating Business Operations**
   - o XYZ Clothing Store integrated its website with a CRM system to manage customer data, track interactions, and streamline its sales and marketing processes.
   - o They utilized project management software and collaboration tools to facilitate seamless communication and workflow management among their remote teams.
   - o By implementing secure user authentication and access control systems, XYZ Clothing Store protected sensitive customer information.
   - o They regularly updated their website's content and functionality to stay relevant, adapting to their target audience's changing needs and preferences.

6. **Enhancing SEO and Visibility**
   - XYZ Clothing Store conducted extensive keyword research and optimized its website's content, improving search engine rankings for relevant fashion-related keywords.
   - By consistently publishing high-quality and informative content, they established themselves as a reliable source of fashion information and attracted a loyal audience.
   - XYZ Clothing Store actively built high-quality backlinks through collaborations with fashion bloggers and influencers, boosting their search engine visibility.
   - They ensured their website was mobile-friendly and optimized for speed, providing a seamless user experience for mobile users and improving their search rankings.

As a result of implementing these strategies, XYZ Clothing Store experienced significant growth in its online sales, brand recognition, and customer loyalty. Their website became a revenue-generating platform, attracting many visitors and converting them into loyal customers. The enhanced customer support, optimized marketing efforts, and streamlined business operations contributed to their success in the highly competitive fashion industry.

This case study demonstrates how an Indian SMB can leverage a robust website to grow, establish their brand, and excel in their industry. By implementing similar strategies tailored to their specific business needs, other Indian SMBs can also unlock their full potential and achieve long-term success in the digital market landscape.

Importance of mobile optimization

In today's digital-first world, mobile optimization is not just a luxury but a necessity. As smartphones become the primary device for online browsing, businesses must prioritize mobile optimization to cater to the ever-growing user base. But what exactly is mobile optimization, and why is it crucial for businesses? Let's explore further.

1. The Rise of Mobile Browsing

Over the past decade, a remarkable and transformative shift has occurred in how people access the internet. With the advent and proliferation of smartphones and the availability of affordable data plans, the number of users relying on their mobile devices for various online activities such as browsing, shopping, and social interaction has witnessed an unprecedented surge. Recent studies conducted by leading experts in the field have provided compelling evidence that mobile devices now contribute to more than 50% of the overall web traffic, solidifying their position as the primary gateway to the digital world. As this upward trajectory shows no signs of slowing down, it is clear that mobile devices will continue to dominate the landscape of internet usage for the foreseeable future.

2. User Experience (UX) is King

Mobile users have unique needs and expectations. In today's fast-paced world, where almost everyone owns a smartphone, websites must cater to the requirements of mobile users. These users demand fast loading times, seamless navigation, and a user interface designed to fit their screens perfectly. When websites are not optimized for mobile devices, users are often forced to pinch and zoom to view the content, which can be frustrating and inconvenient. This suboptimal user experience can lead to high bounce rates and a negative brand perception. On the other hand, when websites provide a positive mobile user experience, it not only increases user engagement but also helps to reduce bounce rates. Furthermore, a satisfying mobile experience can contribute to fostering brand loyalty among mobile users, as they appreciate the effort put into delivering a seamless and tailored experience on their devices.

3. Impact on SEO and Online Visibility

Search engines like Google strongly emphasize the importance of having mobile-optimized websites. Google has introduced a concept called mobile-first indexing, which means that the mobile version of a website's content is given priority when indexing and determining search rankings. This shift in focus towards mobile compatibility is crucial because it directly impacts website visibility and organic search traffic. Therefore, website owners must be mobile-friendly to maintain a higher ranking and increase organic search traffic.

4. Conversion Rates and Mobile Commerce

Mobile commerce, also known as m-commerce, is a rapidly growing trend in the digital world. Today, more and more users find purchasing directly from their smartphones convenient and comfortable. This shift in consumer behavior has paved the way for businesses to optimize their mobile checkout process, leading to a decrease in cart abandonment rates and a significant boost in sales.

When the mobile checkout process is streamlined and user-friendly, it creates a seamless shopping experience for customers. They can easily navigate the purchase journey, select their desired products, and proceed to the payment stage without hassles. This smooth and efficient process not only saves time for users but also instills a sense of trust and security.

On the other hand, if users encounter obstacles or perceive the mobile checkout process as insecure, it can negatively impact their willingness to complete the purchase. Complicated forms, slow loading times, or concerns about data security can all contribute to a higher likelihood of cart abandonment. Therefore, businesses must prioritize optimizing their mobile checkout process, ensuring it is user-friendly, secure, and hassle-free.

In conclusion, the rise of mobile commerce presents tremendous business opportunities, but it also comes with the challenge of providing users with a seamless and secure checkout experience. By understanding the importance of an optimized mobile checkout process and addressing any potential obstacles, businesses can maximize their sales potential and create a loyal customer base in the mobile commerce landscape.

5. Social Media and Mobile Synergy

Social media platforms like Facebook, Instagram, and Twitter are primarily accessed through mobile devices. This widespread usage of mobile devices has made it crucial for businesses to optimize their social media marketing strategies for mobile platforms. By doing so, companies can effectively reach their target audience and capitalize on the growing trend of mobile usage.

In particular, when potential customers click on a product link on Instagram, they have certain expectations. They want to be directed to a landing page designed and optimized for mobile devices. This seamless mobile experience is essential for businesses to provide a positive user experience and increase the likelihood of conversions. Therefore, companies need to invest time and effort into creating mobile-optimized landing pages that align with the design and functionality of popular social media platforms.

6. Staying Ahead of the Competition

In today's highly competitive digital landscape, businesses must recognize the importance of catering to mobile users. By prioritizing mobile optimization, brands can gain a significant advantage over their competitors. This advantage translates into capturing a larger mobile market share and, most importantly, ensuring they take advantage of potential customers whom their rivals might otherwise sway. In a world where almost everyone relies on their mobile devices for various activities, from browsing the internet to shopping online, businesses must recognize the value of catering to this growing market segment. By embracing mobile optimization, brands can stay ahead of the curve and establish a strong presence in the mobile realm, effectively positioning themselves as leaders in their respective industries.

7. Future-Proofing Your Business

With the rapid and ongoing advancements in mobile technology, such as the ever-growing popularity of augmented reality (AR), virtual reality (VR), and the increasing prevalence of voice search, it has become increasingly crucial for businesses to prioritize mobile optimization. By embracing these cutting-edge technologies and optimizing their online presence for mobile devices, companies can effectively future-proof their online interactions and stay ahead of the curve in this digitally driven era.

Conclusion

Mobile optimization is no longer optional but has become an indispensable and vital aspect of a comprehensive digital strategy. In today's fast-paced and technologically advanced world, businesses must recognize and acknowledge the increasing importance of catering to mobile users' unique needs and preferences. By embracing and implementing mobile optimization techniques, companies can create seamless and user-friendly web experiences specifically designed to meet the expectations of mobile users. This proactive approach enhances user engagement and significantly improves conversion rates, increasing sales and revenue. Furthermore, with the rapid advancements and constant changes in the digital landscape, businesses must remain agile, adaptable, and competitive. By prioritizing mobile optimization, companies can stay ahead of the curve and effectively navigate the dynamic and ever-evolving digital terrain, ensuring long-term success and growth.

Walkthrough

Here is a walkthrough for an Indian small and medium-sized business (SMB) on implementing mobile optimization techniques for their website:

1. **Responsive Design**: Ensure that your website has a responsive design that automatically adjusts its layout and elements based on the user's device screen size. This will provide a consistent and user-friendly experience across various mobile devices.
2. **Mobile-Friendly Navigation**: Optimize your website's navigation for mobile users by simplifying menus and using clear, easy-to-tap buttons. Avoid using hover effects that do not work on touchscreens.
3. **Fast Loading Times**: Improve your website's loading speed by compressing images, minifying CSS and JavaScript files, and leveraging browser caching. This will help mobile users access your website quickly, reducing bounce rates.
4. **Optimized Content**: Ensure your website's content is easily readable on mobile devices. Use legible fonts, appropriate font sizes, and sufficient spacing between paragraphs. Break up long paragraphs into smaller chunks for better readability.
5. **Mobile-Friendly Forms**: If your website includes forms for user interaction, optimize them for mobile devices. Use input fields and buttons that are easy to tap, and minimize the number of required fields to streamline the user experience.
6. **Mobile SEO**: Implement mobile SEO best practices to improve your website's visibility on search engines. This includes optimizing meta tags, using descriptive headings, and ensuring your website is included in mobile sitemaps.

7. **Mobile Analytics**: Use mobile analytics tools, such as Google Analytics, to track user behavior and identify areas for improvement. Analyze user flows, bounce rates, and conversions to understand how mobile users interact with your website.

8. **Mobile Payment Integration**: If you offer online transactions, ensure your website integrates with mobile payment gateways popular in India, such as Paytm, PhonePe, or Google Pay. This will provide a seamless and convenient checkout experience for mobile users.

9. **Test and Iterate**: Regularly test your website on various mobile devices and screen sizes to ensure optimal performance and user experience. Solicit feedback from mobile users and make iterative improvements based on their input.

10. **Stay Up-to-Date**: Keep up with the latest mobile optimization trends, technologies, and user behaviors. Continuously monitor industry developments and adapt your mobile optimization strategy accordingly.

By following these steps, an Indian SMB can effectively implement mobile optimization techniques on their website, providing a user-friendly experience for mobile users and maximizing their online presence.

Case Study: Boosting Mobile Conversion Rates for E-Commerce Business

Challenge: An e-commerce business specializing in fashion retail noticed a significant disparity between mobile and desktop conversion rates. While desktop users converted satisfactorily, the mobile conversion rate was alarmingly low. The company realized the need to optimize its mobile experience to capitalize on the growing number of mobile shoppers.

Solution: The company implemented a comprehensive mobile optimization strategy to improve the mobile user experience and boost conversion rates. Here are the key steps they took:

1. Responsive Design: The company revamped its website using a responsive design approach. This ensured their website automatically adjusted its layout and elements to provide a seamless experience across various mobile devices.
2. Mobile-Friendly Navigation: They simplified their website's navigation for mobile users by streamlining menus and using clear, easy-to-tap buttons. They eliminated hover effects that don't work on touchscreens, ensuring smooth navigation.
3. Enhanced Loading Speed: The company optimized its website's loading speed by compressing images, minifying CSS and JavaScript files, and leveraging browser caching. This significantly improved the loading time, reducing bounce rates.
4. Optimized Content: They optimized their website's content for mobile devices using legible fonts, appropriate font sizes, and sufficient paragraph spacing. They broke up long paragraphs into smaller chunks for better readability.
5. Streamlined Checkout Process: The company optimized its mobile checkout process, simplifying forms and reducing the required fields. They integrated popular mobile payment gateways to facilitate a seamless and convenient checkout experience.

Results: The mobile optimization efforts yielded remarkable results for the e-commerce business:

- Mobile Conversion Rate Increase: The company saw a significant increase in its mobile conversion rate, aligning it more closely with its desktop conversion rate. The improved mobile experience led to more successful purchases from mobile users.
- Reduced Bounce Rates: The streamlined mobile experience resulted in reduced bounce rates. Users were more engaged and less likely to abandon their shopping due to frustration or inconvenience.
- Increased Revenue: As the mobile conversion rate improved, the business experienced a notable boost in revenue from mobile sales. The optimized mobile experience allowed them to capture a larger share of the growing mobile market.
- Enhanced Brand Perception: By prioritizing mobile optimization, the company enhanced its brand perception among mobile users. The seamless and user-friendly mobile experience created a positive impression and fostered brand loyalty.

Concluding Thoughts: This case study demonstrates the significant impact of mobile optimization on an e-commerce business. The company successfully improved its mobile conversion rate, reduced bounce rates, and increased revenue by implementing a comprehensive mobile optimization strategy. The enhanced mobile experience resulted in more successful purchases and strengthened their brand image among mobile users. Embracing mobile optimization proved to be a crucial step in staying competitive in the mobile commerce landscape.

Utilizing cloud storage and applications

The shift from physical storage solutions and traditional software to cloud-based platforms has revolutionized businesses' operations. By leveraging the cloud, companies can now access scalable storage capabilities and application solutions that can be easily accessed anywhere. This enables them to streamline their operations and opens up opportunities for small and medium-sized businesses (SMBs) to enhance their growth and efficiency.

Cloud-based platforms offer a wide range of specific features and benefits that can significantly benefit SMBs. For instance, these platforms provide flexible and customizable storage options to meet each business's unique needs. Whether it's storing large amounts of data or securely backing up essential files, the cloud has covered it.

Moreover, cloud-based applications offer many possibilities for SMBs to optimize their processes and workflows. From project management tools to collaboration platforms, these applications enable teams to work seamlessly, regardless of their physical location. This enhances productivity and fosters innovation and creativity within the organization.

In addition, the cloud offers enhanced data security measures, ensuring that sensitive business information is safeguarded against potential threats. With advanced encryption techniques and robust access controls, SMBs can have peace of mind knowing that their data is protected.

The shift to cloud-based platforms has brought about a paradigm shift in how businesses operate. It has provided SMBs with the tools and capabilities they need to compete in today's digital landscape. By embracing the cloud, companies can unlock new opportunities, drive growth, and improve efficiency in previously unimaginable ways. So, if you haven't already, it's time to explore the world of cloud computing and see how it can transform your business.

1. Understanding the Cloud

Before diving into applications, it is essential to have a comprehensive understanding of the cloud. Cloud computing is storing and accessing data and programs over the internet, eliminating the need for local storage on a computer's hard drive or a local server. By utilizing expansive remote server networks, cloud computing enables the processing, management, and storage of data in an efficient and scalable manner.

Furthermore, the cloud offers numerous benefits to individuals and organizations. It provides flexibility by allowing users to access their data and applications from anywhere with an internet connection. Collaboration becomes seamless as multiple users can work on the same document simultaneously, regardless of their physical location. The cloud also ensures data security and disaster recovery, as data is stored redundantly across multiple servers.

Additionally, cloud computing offers cost savings by eliminating the need for expensive hardware and infrastructure. Users can scale their computing resources up or down based on their requirements, paying only for the resources they use. This scalability enables businesses to adapt to changing demands quickly and handle peak workloads without disruptions.

In summary, understanding the cloud is crucial before exploring its applications. Cloud computing revolutionizes how data is stored, accessed, and managed, providing flexibility, collaboration, security, and cost savings to individuals and organizations.

2. Benefits of Cloud Storage

- **Scalability**: Unlike physical storage solutions, cloud storage enables businesses to scale up or down according to their needs without substantial upfront costs.
- **Accessibility**: Data stored in the cloud can be accessed from anywhere with an internet connection, facilitating remote work and global collaboration.
- **Security**: Reputable cloud providers heavily invest in security measures, including data encryption, multi-factor authentication, and regular backups.
- **Cost Efficiency**: Businesses can avoid expenses for maintaining and upgrading physical servers.

3. Embracing Cloud Applications

Cloud applications, also called cloud apps, are becoming increasingly popular in today's digital landscape. These software solutions offer users the convenience of accessing and interacting with the server, data storage, and software through the Internet. With an internet connection, users can work on their documents, spreadsheets, and presentations from any device. Not only do cloud apps provide flexibility and accessibility, but they also offer seamless collaboration among team members. With cloud applications like Google Workspace, Microsoft Office 365, and Salesforce, users can easily share files, edit documents in real-time, and communicate effectively within their organizations. Embracing cloud technology has become essential for businesses and individuals alike, enabling them to streamline their workflows, enhance productivity, and stay connected in today's fast-paced world.

Advantages:

- **Automatic Updates**: Cloud apps update automatically, ensuring businesses have the latest features and security patches.
- **Collaboration**: Many cloud apps facilitate real-time collaboration, allowing multiple users to edit documents or work on projects simultaneously.
- **Subscription-Based**: This allows businesses to utilize premium software solutions without incurring high upfront costs.

4. Integration Capabilities

One of the cloud's most influential and advantageous features is its remarkable ability to integrate and connect various applications seamlessly. This highly interconnected ecosystem enhances productivity and efficiency by facilitating the seamless integration of different software solutions. For instance, customer relationship management (CRM) software can be effortlessly integrated with cutting-edge email marketing tools, enabling businesses to effectively manage and nurture customer relationships while executing targeted marketing campaigns. Additionally, accounting software can seamlessly sync with popular e-commerce platforms, ensuring accurate financial tracking and streamlined order management. The cloud's versatility and adaptability empower businesses to harness their software tools' full potential, revolutionizing their operations and maximizing their overall performance.

5. Data Backup and Disaster Recovery

Utilizing cloud storage offers several benefits. One of the key advantages is the automatic backups it provides for essential data. This means that even in the event of local hardware failures, natural disasters, or any other unforeseen circumstances, you can rest assured that your data will remain intact and recoverable. This level of reliability is crucial for businesses and individuals alike, as it eliminates the risk of losing valuable information. Additionally, cloud storage provides the convenience of accessing your data from anywhere, anytime, as long as you have an internet connection. This flexibility allows for seamless collaboration and remote work, empowering teams to work effectively without being tied to a specific location. Furthermore, cloud storage often offers scalable solutions, meaning you can quickly increase or decrease your storage capacity based on your needs. This ensures that you only pay for the storage you use, making it a cost-effective option for businesses of all sizes. In summary, by utilizing cloud storage, you not only guarantee the safety and recoverability of your data but also gain the benefits of accessibility, flexibility, and scalability that can significantly enhance productivity and efficiency.

6. Navigating Security Concerns

While cloud providers prioritize security, it is essential for businesses to actively participate in ensuring a secure environment. In addition to the mentioned practices, companies should consider implementing the following measures:

- Conduct regular security audits and risk assessments to identify potential vulnerabilities and address them promptly.
- Establish clear security policies and procedures outlining best data protection and privacy practices.
- We provide ongoing training and awareness programs to educate employees about the latest security threats and best practices.
- We are implementing robust access controls and monitoring systems to prevent unauthorized access to sensitive information.
- We are collaborating with cloud providers to ensure the implementation of industry-standard security measures and protocols.
- We are regularly reviewing and updating security measures to stay ahead of evolving threats and vulnerabilities.

By actively engaging in these practices, businesses can enhance their overall security posture and mitigate the risks associated with cloud-based operations.

7. Making the Transition

For businesses new to the cloud, the transition might seem daunting. However, with careful planning and execution, this transition can be a smooth and successful process. Here are some steps to consider:

1. **Assessment:** It is essential to carefully assess and analyze which data and applications would benefit most from moving to the cloud. Businesses can prioritize their transition efforts and maximize their benefits by identifying the key areas where the cloud can provide the most significant value.

2. **Training**: To ensure a successful transition, providing employees with the necessary training and support is crucial. This will help them understand how to use new cloud tools and technologies effectively, enabling them to work efficiently and maximize the cloud resources.

3. **Pilot Programs**: Before making a full-scale transition, businesses can run pilot programs to test the waters and gain valuable insights. These pilot programs will help identify potential challenges or issues during the transition process. Companies can mitigate risks and ensure a smoother transition by addressing these challenges early on.

4. **Monitoring and Evaluation**: Once the transition to the cloud is underway, it is essential to continually monitor and evaluate the performance and impact of the cloud infrastructure. This will allow businesses to make necessary adjustments and optimizations, ensuring that they maximize the benefits of the cloud and achieve their desired outcomes.

By following these steps and taking a systematic approach, businesses can successfully navigate the transition to the cloud and unlock its full potential.

8. The Future of Cloud Computing

The potential of cloud computing is immense. It constantly evolves with emerging technologies such as edge computing, AI integration, and quantum computing, all poised to revolutionize the cloud landscape. These advancements open up new possibilities and opportunities for small and medium-sized businesses (SMBs) that embrace and adapt to these innovations. By staying ahead of the curve and leveraging these cutting-edge technologies, SMBs can position themselves as industry leaders, driving growth and success in their respective fields.

Conclusion

Cloud storage and applications have become indispensable in today's business landscape. They have revolutionized organizations' operations, providing unprecedented opportunities for efficiency, collaboration, and growth. With the ability to securely store and access data from anywhere, businesses can streamline their operations and optimize their workflows. Moreover, cloud-based applications offer various functionalities that enhance productivity and enable seamless collaboration among team members. By leveraging these powerful tools, small and medium-sized businesses (SMBs) can stay competitive in an increasingly digital world, adapt to rapidly evolving market demands, and unlock new avenues for growth and success.

To implement cloud storage and applications in an Indian SMB, follow these steps:

1. **Assess Your Needs**: Evaluate your business requirements and identify areas where cloud storage and applications can bring the most value. Consider factors such as data storage, collaboration needs, and scalability.
2. **Choose a Cloud Service Provider**: Research and select a reliable cloud service provider that offers storage and application solutions tailored to SMBs. Consider data security, pricing, customer support, and the provider's track record.
3. **Plan Data Migration**: Determine which data needs to be migrated to the cloud and create a migration plan. Ensure that data is transferred securely and without interruptions to minimize downtime.

4. **Train Employees**: Train your employees on effectively using cloud storage and applications. Educate them on data security best practices, collaboration features, and accessing data remotely.

5. **Implement Cloud Storage**: Set up cloud storage for your business data. Organize files and folders logically to ensure easy access and efficient collaboration. Enable appropriate access controls and permissions to protect sensitive data.

6. **Explore Cloud Applications**: Identify cloud applications that can benefit your SMB. For example, consider using productivity suites like Google Workspace or Microsoft Office 365 for document creation and collaboration. Look for industry-specific applications that can streamline your business processes.

7. **Integrate Cloud Applications**: Integrate cloud applications with your existing systems, such as customer relationship management (CRM) or accounting software. This integration will ensure smooth data flow and optimize your workflows.

8. **Ensure Data Security**: Implement security measures to protect your data in the cloud. This includes using strong passwords, enabling multi-factor authentication, and regularly updating security settings. Regularly backup your data to prevent loss and ensure business continuity.

9. **Monitor and Optimize**: Continuously monitor the performance of your cloud storage and applications. Identify areas for improvement and optimize your workflows to maximize efficiency and productivity.

10. **Stay Updated**: Stay informed about the latest cloud storage and application trends and updates. Regularly evaluate your cloud service provider's offerings to ensure they meet your evolving needs.

By following these steps, an Indian SMB can effectively implement cloud storage and applications, enabling them to streamline operations, enhance collaboration, and drive growth in their business.

Case Study: XYZ Company's Transition to Cloud Computing

Background

XYZ Company, a leading IT solutions provider, faced challenges managing their growing data storage needs and ensuring seamless collaboration among their remote teams. They recognized the need to adopt cloud computing to overcome these hurdles and improve operational efficiency.

Objectives

- Enhance data storage and accessibility.
- Improve collaboration and communication among teams.
- Strengthen data security and disaster recovery capabilities.
- Streamline workflows and optimize resource utilization.

Solution

XYZ Company partnered with a reputable cloud service provider to implement a comprehensive cloud computing solution. The solution included the following components:

1. **Cloud Storage:** The company migrated its data from traditional physical storage to the cloud. This enabled them to securely store and access their data from anywhere, eliminating the need for local servers.

2. **Collaboration Tools**: XYZ Company adopted cloud-based collaboration tools like project management platforms and real-time document editing and sharing applications. These tools allowed their teams to collaborate seamlessly, regardless of their physical location.

3. **Data Security Measures**: The cloud service provider implemented robust security measures, including data encryption, multi-factor authentication, and regular backups. This ensured that XYZ Company's data remained protected from unauthorized access and potential threats.

4. **Scalability and Flexibility**: The cloud solution allowed XYZ Company to scale its storage and computing resources based on evolving needs. This flexibility allowed them to handle peak workloads and adapt to changing demands without disruptions.

Results

By transitioning to cloud computing, XYZ Company experienced significant improvements in its operations and overall efficiency:

1. **Enhanced Data Accessibility**: The cloud-based storage solution enabled employees to access critical data and files from anywhere, facilitating remote work and improving team collaboration.

2. **Streamlined Workflows**: The adoption of cloud-based collaboration tools streamlined internal processes and improved communication among team members. This led to increased productivity and faster project completion times.

3. **Improved Data Security**: The robust security measures implemented by the cloud service provider ensured that XYZ Company's data remained protected against potential threats.

This instilled confidence among their clients and strengthened their reputation as a trusted IT solutions provider.

4. **Cost Savings**: By eliminating the need for physical storage infrastructure and reducing maintenance costs, XYZ Company achieved significant cost savings. They were able to allocate their resources more efficiently, investing in other areas of their business.

Conclusion

XYZ Company's successful transition to cloud computing resolved their data storage and collaboration challenges and provided them with a competitive edge in the market. By leveraging the benefits of cloud storage and applications, they enhanced their operational efficiency, improved data security, and achieved cost savings. This case study exemplifies how businesses can leverage cloud computing to overcome obstacles and drive growth in today's digital landscape.

MASTERING DIGITAL MARKETING

Exploring platforms like Google, Facebook, Instagram, and LinkedIn

The digital landscape offers various platforms that provide businesses unique opportunities to connect with their target audiences, effectively promote their products and services, and successfully grow and establish their brand presence. Among these platforms, Google, Facebook, Instagram, and LinkedIn are particularly noteworthy, as each platform serves a distinct and valuable role in digital marketing. Now, let's delve into the specific offerings and potential benefits businesses can harness from each platform to maximize their online presence and achieve their marketing goals.

1. Google: More than a Search Engine

Google is not just a search engine; it offers a range of powerful tools and services that can benefit businesses in various ways. Here are some key features and benefits of utilizing Google:

- **Search Engine Optimization (SEO):** By optimizing your website for organic search, you can improve its visibility and credibility. This means that when users search for relevant keywords, your website will appear higher in the search results, increasing the chances of attracting organic traffic.

- **Google Ads**: Besides organic search, Google also offers a paid advertising platform called Google Ads. With Google Ads, you can target specific audiences based on their interests, demographics, and search behavior. You can enhance your visibility and drive more conversions to your website by running targeted ad campaigns.
- **Google My Business**: For local businesses, Google My Business is a valuable tool. It allows you to manage your online presence on Google, ensuring that accurate and up-to-date information is displayed when users search for your business. You can provide essential details such as your location, operating hours, contact information, and even collect customer reviews. This helps in establishing trust and attracting potential customers in your local area.

These are just a few examples of how Google offers more than just a search engine. By leveraging these tools effectively, businesses can significantly benefit from increased visibility, credibility, and targeted advertising opportunities.

2. Facebook: Building Communities and Engaging Audiences

In today's digital landscape, having a solid online presence is crucial for businesses. One of the most effective platforms for achieving this is Facebook. With its diverse features, Facebook offers various ways for businesses to connect with their target audience and build a loyal community. Let's explore some key aspects of Facebook that can help companies to thrive:

- **Facebook Pages**: Facebook Pages provide businesses with a dedicated space to establish their digital identity. Here, companies can showcase their products or services, share valuable content, and engage with their followers. By consistently updating their Facebook Page with relevant and engaging posts, businesses can stay connected with their audience and foster a sense of community.

- **Facebook Ads**: Facebook Ads is a powerful advertising tool that allows businesses to run targeted ad campaigns. With access to detailed demographic information, businesses can reach potential customers who match their target audience. Companies can maximize their reach and increase brand awareness by creating compelling ad content and utilizing Facebook's advanced targeting options.

- **Facebook Groups**: Facebook Groups offer a unique opportunity for businesses to connect with their audience on a more personal level. Businesses can create or join relevant groups to nurture communities and interact directly with customers. This allows companies to build stronger relationships with their audience and provides valuable insights through market research and feedback gathering.

- **Facebook Marketplace**: It is an ideal platform for businesses showcasing their products and connecting with potential buyers. With millions of users actively browsing and searching for products, companies can list their offerings and reach a wider audience. Whether selling physical products or promoting services, Facebook Marketplace provides businesses with a convenient and effective way to expand their customer base.

By leveraging the power of Facebook's features, businesses can truly engage their audience, build loyal communities, and drive growth. Whether through Facebook Pages, targeted ad campaigns, user groups, or the Marketplace, businesses have many opportunities to make a lasting impact in the digital world.

3. Instagram: Visual Storytelling and Brand Aesthetics

- **Instagram Feed**: Share visually captivating images and videos that convey your brand's narrative and deeply connect with your target audience.
- **Instagram Stories**: Incorporate temporary and exclusive content to promote your brand, offer behind-the-scenes sneak peeks, or engage in interactive polls and Q&A sessions with your followers.
- **Instagram Reels**: Embrace the popular trend of short videos to produce highly captivating and shareable content that has the potential to go viral and amplify your brand's reach.
- **Instagram Shop**: Seamlessly integrate and enhance your e-commerce experience by featuring a curated selection of your products directly on your Instagram profile, providing a convenient and visually appealing way for your audience to explore and make purchases.

4. LinkedIn Professional Networking and B2B Marketing

LinkedIn is a robust platform that offers various features to help businesses establish their presence and reach a wider audience. Here are some key strategies you can implement on LinkedIn:

- **Company Pages**: Create a compelling Company Page to showcase your business's achievements, services, and culture. This is an opportunity to engage with your target audience and build brand awareness.

- **LinkedIn Ads**: Use LinkedIn's advertising options to target professionals relevant to your industry. With LinkedIn Ads, you can refine your audience based on industry, job title, and more factors. This allows you to reach the right people with your marketing messages.
- **LinkedIn Articles**: Demonstrate your expertise and thought leadership by publishing in-depth articles directly on your LinkedIn profile. This helps you establish authority in your industry and allows you to share valuable insights with your network.
- **LinkedIn Groups**: Engaging in discussions and industry-specific groups can be a valuable way to network and connect with like-minded professionals. By actively participating in these groups, you can establish yourself as an authority figure in your field and gain visibility among your target audience.

5. Cross-Platform Strategies

- **Consistent Branding**: Maintaining a consistent brand voice, aesthetic, and messaging across all platforms is essential. This helps to create a cohesive and recognizable brand identity that resonates with your target audience.
- **Integrated Campaigns**: Running integrated campaigns that span multiple platforms can significantly increase your reach and engagement. By leveraging different channels and mediums, you can effectively communicate your message to a broader audience and achieve better results.
- **Analytics and Insights**: Each platform provides valuable tools and metrics to analyze the performance of your campaigns. By understanding these analytics and gaining insights into user behavior and preferences, you can refine your strategies and

make data-driven decisions to optimize your returns on investment.

6. Navigating Challenges

While these platforms offer immense opportunities, there are several challenges that businesses may encounter:

- **Algorithm Changes**: Platforms regularly update their algorithms, which can significantly impact the visibility and engagement of businesses. Therefore, companies must stay informed about these changes and adjust their strategies accordingly to maintain their online presence and reach their target audience effectively.
- **Privacy Concerns**: In today's digital age, data privacy has become a significant concern for individuals and businesses. Businesses must prioritize transparency and ethical practices in advertising, ensuring customer data is handled securely and responsibly.
- **Platform Saturation**: With the proliferation of online businesses, competition for attention and customer engagement has become increasingly fierce. Companies must employ creative and authentic strategies that resonate with their audience to stand out. Understanding their target audience's preferences, needs, and behaviors is essential to cut through the noise and capture their attention effectively.

In summary, while these platforms present tremendous business opportunities, knowing and navigating the challenges associated with algorithm changes, privacy concerns, and platform saturation is essential. By staying informed, prioritizing ethical practices, and crafting engaging strategies, businesses can overcome these challenges and thrive in the digital landscape.

7. Staying Updated, Adaptable, and Proactive

In today's rapidly changing digital landscape, businesses must stay ahead of the curve. Here are some strategies to consider:

- **Embracing Emerging Features**: Stay on top of the latest trends and updates on platforms like Instagram and LinkedIn. For example, be an early adopter of new features like Reels or Live videos, which can give you a competitive advantage and help you reach a wider audience.
- **Understanding and Adapting to Shifts in User Behavior**: User preferences and behaviors constantly evolve. Businesses need to monitor these changes and adjust their strategies accordingly. By staying attuned to the needs and preferences of your target audience, you can tailor your marketing efforts to reach and engage with them effectively.
- **Continued Learning and Knowledge Expansion**: In such a dynamic landscape, staying informed and up-to-date with industry trends and best practices is essential. Attend webinars, workshops, or conferences related to your industry. Subscribe to platform-specific blogs or newsletters to receive regular updates. Engage in online communities or forums to learn from industry experts and exchange ideas with peers.

By adopting a proactive approach and embracing these strategies, businesses can stay ahead of the competition and adapt to the ever-changing digital environment.

Conclusion

Google, Facebook, Instagram, LinkedIn, and other popular social media platforms provide unique and valuable opportunities for businesses to grow, engage with their target audience, and convert leads into customers. These platforms offer various features and tools that can be leveraged to enhance a comprehensive digital marketing strategy.

For instance, Google, being the most widely used search engine globally, allows businesses to increase their online visibility through search engine optimization (SEO) techniques and targeted advertising campaigns. This enables companies to reach potential customers actively searching for products or services related to their industry.

With its vast user base and advanced targeting options, Facebook allows businesses to create highly personalized and engaging advertisements. Companies can reach specific demographics and interests by utilizing Facebook's detailed audience targeting capabilities, ensuring the right people see their ads.

Instagram, known for its visual-centric nature, provides businesses with a platform to showcase their products or services creatively. Through high-quality visuals, businesses can captivate their audience and build brand awareness. Instagram's features, such as Stories and IGTV, allow companies to engage with their followers more interactively and authentically.

LinkedIn, a professional networking platform, offers businesses the chance to connect with industry professionals, establish thought leadership, and build valuable business relationships. By sharing insightful content, participating in industry-specific groups, and utilizing LinkedIn's advertising options, businesses can position themselves as industry leaders and attract potential clients.

By strategically integrating these platforms into a comprehensive digital marketing strategy, businesses can effectively navigate the digital realm, reach their target audience across different channels, and ultimately achieve measurable success in brand awareness, lead generation, and customer conversions.

Walkthrough: Exploring Platforms for an Indian SMB

As an Indian small and medium-sized business (SMB) looking to explore the platforms mentioned in this topic, here's a step-by-step walkthrough to get started:

1. **Identify your target audience and goals**: Determine who your target audience is and what you aim to achieve through your digital marketing efforts. Are you looking to increase brand awareness, drive website traffic, or generate leads? Understanding your goals will help you choose the most appropriate platforms and strategies.

2. **Google**: Begin by optimizing your website for search engines. Research relevant keywords related to your business and industry and incorporate them into your website's content. This will help improve your website's visibility in organic search results. Consider utilizing Google Ads to run targeted ad campaigns and reach potential customers actively searching for products or services similar to yours. Additionally, create a Google My Business listing to enhance your local presence and provide accurate information to potential customers.

3. **Facebook**: Create a Facebook Page for your business and fill it with engaging content that resonates with your target

audience. Regularly update your page with posts, including product/service highlights, customer testimonials, and industry-related news. Utilize Facebook Ads to reach specific demographics and interests relevant to your business. Experiment with different ad formats and messaging to find the best for your target audience.

4. **Instagram**: Establish an Instagram business account and focus on visually appealing content that showcases your products or services. Use high-quality images and videos to tell your brand's story and engage your target audience. Post regularly and utilize features like Instagram Stories and Reels to provide behind-the-scenes glimpses, conduct interactive polls, and share captivating short videos. Utilize Instagram Shop to make it easy for your audience to explore and purchase your offerings.

5. **LinkedIn**: Create a professional LinkedIn Company Page for your business. Showcase your company's achievements, services, and culture. Share industry insights and valuable content through LinkedIn Articles to establish thought leadership. Join relevant LinkedIn Groups and engage in discussions to network with like-minded professionals and gain visibility among your target audience. Use LinkedIn Ads to reach professionals pertinent to your industry and refine your target audience based on industry, job titles, and more.

6. **Cross-Platform Strategies**: Maintain consistent branding across all platforms to create a cohesive brand identity. Integrate your campaigns by cross-promoting your content and leveraging the strengths of each platform. Analyze the performance of your campaigns using analytics tools provided by each forum to make data-driven decisions and optimize your marketing efforts.

7. **Stay Updated and Adapt**: Keep up with each platform's latest trends and updates. Embrace emerging features and adapt your strategies to shifts in user behavior. Continuously expand your knowledge and stay informed about industry best practices through webinars, workshops, and online communities.

Remember, the key to success is understanding your target audience, setting clear goals, and tailoring your strategies accordingly. Regularly monitor the performance of your campaigns, make adjustments as needed, and stay proactive in exploring new opportunities to grow your online presence and achieve your marketing objectives.

Following this walkthrough and continuously refining your digital marketing strategies, your Indian SMB can effectively explore and leverage the platforms mentioned to connect with your target audience, establish your brand presence, and drive business growth.

Case Study: XYZ Company's Successful Digital Marketing Campaign

XYZ Company, a leading e-commerce retailer specializing in fashion accessories, recently executed a highly successful digital marketing campaign utilizing various platforms like Google, Facebook, Instagram, and LinkedIn. The campaign aimed to increase brand awareness, drive website traffic, and boost sales.

1. **Google**: XYZ Company implemented a comprehensive search engine optimization (SEO) strategy to improve their website's organic search visibility. They conducted thorough keyword research and optimized their website's content, meta tags, and URLs with relevant keywords. They also utilized Google Ads to run targeted ad campaigns, focusing on product-specific

keywords and utilizing ad extensions to showcase promotions and discounts. Combining SEO and Google Ads increased website traffic and improved conversion rates.

2. **Facebook**: XYZ Company created a captivating Facebook Page that showcased their latest fashion accessories, behind-the-scenes content, and exclusive promotions. They regularly posted engaging content, including high-quality images and videos, to keep their audience informed and entertained. They also utilized Facebook Ads to target specific demographics and interests, increasing brand visibility and website traffic. By leveraging Facebook's detailed analytics, XYZ Company optimized its ad campaigns and identified the most effective ad formats and messaging.

3. **Instagram**: XYZ Company leveraged Instagram's visual storytelling capabilities to showcase its fashion accessories in a visually appealing and aspirational manner. They created a consistent brand aesthetic by curating a visually cohesive Instagram feed that resonated with their target audience. They utilized Instagram Stories to provide behind-the-scenes glimpses of their products, conducted interactive polls and Q&A sessions to engage with their followers, and utilized Instagram Reels to create short, shareable videos that showcased their latest collections. This resulted in increased brand engagement, follower growth, and website traffic.

4. **LinkedIn**: XYZ Company established a strong presence on LinkedIn by creating a Company Page highlighting their industry expertise and values. They regularly published in-depth articles that provided valuable insights into the fashion accessory industry, positioning themselves as thought leaders. They engaged with industry-specific LinkedIn Groups, actively participating in discussions and networking with professionals.

Additionally, they utilized LinkedIn Ads to target professionals in relevant industries and refined their audience based on job titles and company size. This resulted in increased brand credibility, lead generation, and B2B partnerships.

XYZ Company achieved remarkable results by strategically integrating these platforms and tailoring their content and advertising strategies to each platform's strengths. They experienced a significant increase in brand awareness, website traffic, and sales. The campaign's success was primarily attributed to the cohesive branding, personalized targeting, engaging content, and data-driven optimization implemented across all platforms.

Through continuous monitoring and analysis of campaign performance, XYZ Company was able to identify trends, adjust its strategies, and allocate resources effectively. This proactive approach ensured they stayed ahead of the competition and maintained a solid online presence.

This case study illustrates the power of leveraging multiple platforms in a comprehensive digital marketing campaign. By understanding their target audience, setting clear goals, and utilizing each platform's unique features and advantages, businesses can achieve significant growth and success in today's digital landscape.

The role of email marketing and content marketing

In today's rapidly evolving landscape of marketing technologies and platforms, it's crucial to recognize the enduring significance of two tried-and-true strategies that continue to shape digital engagement: email marketing and content marketing. While the digital realm continues to evolve, these timeless strategies remain steadfast in connecting with audiences on a deeper level, fostering trust, and cultivating long-lasting relationships. By implementing a comprehensive marketing strategy incorporating these two pivotal approaches, businesses can deliver value directly to their target audience while establishing a solid foundation of trust and loyalty. Now, let's delve deeper into the pivotal roles that email marketing and content marketing play in the ever-changing world of digital marketing.

1. Email Marketing: Effective Communication with Your Target Audience

- **Building a List**: By actively cultivating a list of interested users, you can establish a direct line of communication with an audience that has already shown interest in your brand.
- **Segmentation and Personalization**: Segmentation techniques allow you to tailor your communication based on

specific demographics or preferences, resulting in higher open rates, increased engagement, and improved conversion rates.

- **Automated Campaigns**: Implementing automated campaigns, such as drip campaigns, enables you to nurture leads over time and guide them through the sales funnel automatically, saving time and effort.
- **Metrics and Analysis**: Regularly monitoring key metrics, such as open rates, click-through rates, and conversion rates, provides valuable insights into the performance of your email campaigns and helps identify areas for enhancement and optimization.
- **Continuous Improvement**: By analyzing campaign performance and making data-driven adjustments, you can continually refine your email marketing strategies to achieve even better results.

2. Content Marketing: Building Authority and Trust

- **Blogs and Articles**: Consistently publishing well-researched and informative content demonstrates expertise and addresses user queries, improving SEO rankings.
- **Infographics and Visual Content**: Visual content can simplify complex subjects, making them more accessible for comprehension and sharing.
- **Videos**: Whether instructional videos or customer testimonials, videos provide a dynamic medium to effectively communicate messages and connect with audiences.
- **E-books and Whitepapers**: In-depth and comprehensive content in e-books and whitepapers can serve as valuable lead magnets, enticing users to provide their email addresses in exchange for valuable insights and knowledge.

- **Webinars and Podcasts**: Engaging audiences through interactive webinars and informative podcasts can establish thought leadership and foster deeper connections with the target audience.

3. Symbiosis: Email and Content Marketing Together

- **Newsletter Value**: Email marketing can be a powerful tool to share recent blog posts, videos, or other content pieces and provide additional context and insights that may not be available on your website. By incorporating email marketing into your content strategy, you can drive traffic back to your website and keep your audience engaged.
- **Exclusive Content**: One way to add value to your email subscribers is by offering them particular articles, guides, or insights that are exclusively available. This creates a sense of exclusivity and makes being on your mailing list more desirable.
- **Feedback Loop**: Emails can serve as a valuable channel for gathering feedback on your content. By including surveys, polls, or simply encouraging your subscribers to reply with their thoughts, you can gain valuable insights into what resonates with your audience and what doesn't. This feedback loop allows you to continuously improve and tailor your content to meet the needs and preferences of your audience.

4. Enhancing Engagement and Building Relationships

- **Value First**: One of the critical strategies for enhancing engagement and building relationships is to prioritize delivering value to users. By providing valuable content, products, or services, you can establish trust and position your brand as a reliable resource that customers can rely on.

- **Nurturing Leads**: Another critical aspect of this strategy is nurturing leads. This involves guiding potential customers from their initial touchpoint with your brand to the final conversion. One effective way to do this is through targeted emails that provide relevant information and resources to help potential customers make informed decisions. Creating and sharing content that guides customers throughout their journey can also be beneficial in nurturing leads.

- **Community Building**: Regular and valuable communication is essential to foster community and loyalty among your audience. This can include sharing updates, insights, and exclusive content with your audience through various channels such as social media, email newsletters, and community forums. By building a solid community, you can create a loyal customer base that advocates for your brand and helps spread the word about your products or services.

5. Challenges and Best Practices

- **Content Overload**: In today's digital landscape, where there is an overwhelming amount of online content, it has become increasingly challenging to capture and retain the attention of your target audience. Creating original, high-quality, and relevant content that provides unique value to your audience is crucial to stand out.

- **Email Deliverability**: When it comes to email marketing, one of the biggest obstacles is ensuring that your emails reach the intended recipients' inboxes and avoid being flagged as spam. To overcome this challenge, it is essential to implement a combination of technical fixes, such as proper email authentication and sender reputation management, along with maintaining a solid level of user engagement. By consistently delivering valuable and engaging content to your subscribers, you can improve your email deliverability rates and increase the chances of your messages being read and acted upon.

- **Adherence to Regulations:** In today's digital age, various regulations are in place to protect individuals' privacy and ensure responsible email marketing practices. Two prominent regulations businesses must comply with are the General Data Protection Regulation (GDPR) and the Controlling the Assault of Non-Solicited Pornography And Marketing (CAN-SPAM) Act. It is essential to familiarize yourself with these regulations and ensure that you have proper consent from individuals before sending them marketing emails. Additionally, providing easy options for individuals to unsubscribe from your email list is a legal requirement and a best practice that helps maintain a positive brand reputation and user experience.

6. The Future of Email and Content Marketing

In today's fast-paced digital world, the future of email and content marketing is constantly evolving. As we embrace technological advancements, we expect to see exciting changes to revolutionize how we interact with emails and consume content. Here are some key trends to watch out for:

- **Interactive Emails:** Email technology is evolving rapidly, opening up new possibilities for creating interactive elements within emails. The options are. Endless, from interactive surveys and quizzes to image carousels. By incorporating interactive features, businesses can enhance user engagement and make their emails more memorable.

- **AI and Personalization**: Artificial Intelligence (AI) transforms how we interact with content. With the help of AI algorithms, marketers can now predict and automate content delivery based on user behavior and preferences. By analyzing user data, AI can tailor content to each individual, creating a highly personalized experience. This level of personalization improves engagement and fosters more robust relationships between businesses and their customers.

- **Voice Search and Content**: The rise of voice-activated devices and virtual assistants has led to a growing trend in voice search. People now use their voice to search for information, make inquiries, and even shop online. As a result, optimizing content for voice search has become crucial for businesses to stay competitive. By understanding how people phrase their voice search queries and optimizing content accordingly, marketers can ensure their content is easily discoverable in voice search results.

In conclusion, the future of email and content marketing is bright and full of exciting possibilities. By embracing interactive emails, leveraging AI for personalization, and optimizing content for voice search, businesses can stay ahead of the curve and deliver engaging experiences to their audience.

7. Continuous Learning and Adapting

Learning and adapting continuously is crucial to ensure email and content marketing success. Here are some key strategies to consider:

- **Stay Updated**: Keep yourself informed about the latest trends and technologies in email and content marketing. This will help you stay ahead of the curve and ensure your strategies are up-to-date.
- **Feedback and Iteration**: Collect feedback from your audience and analyze analytics to gain insights into the effectiveness of your email and content marketing efforts. Use this information to make informed decisions and iterate your strategies accordingly.
- **Innovate**: Embrace innovation and be open to trying new content formats or email strategies. Experimentation lets you discover what resonates with your audience and can lead to breakthrough results.

By implementing these approaches, you can continuously improve your email and content marketing strategies, adapting to the ever-evolving landscape and maximizing your success.

Conclusion

Email marketing and content marketing are like two pillars supporting the edifice of a brand's digital presence. While they operate in different domains, their intertwined nature amplifies the efficacy of each. Businesses can foster genuine connections, establish authority, and drive sustained growth by leveraging their combined strengths.

Sure! Here's a walkthrough on how an Indian SMB can include email marketing and content marketing in their business:

1. **Define Your Target Audience**: Start by identifying your target audience. Determine their demographics, interests, and pain

points. This will help you create content that resonates with them and tailor your email marketing campaigns accordingly.

2. **Build an Email List**: Create opportunities for visitors to your website to subscribe to your email list. Offer valuable content or incentives in exchange for their email addresses. You can also promote your email list on social media and other marketing channels.

3. **Segment Your Email List**: Divide your email list into segments based on location, interests, or purchase history. This lets you send targeted emails more relevant to each piece, increasing engagement and conversion rates.

4. **Create Engaging Content**: Develop a content marketing strategy that aligns with your target audience's interests and needs. Create high-quality blog posts, videos, infographics, or other forms of content that provide value and establish your expertise.

5. **Optimize for SEO**: Optimize your website and content for search engines to improve your visibility in search results. Research keywords relevant to your business and incorporate them naturally into your content, meta tags, and URLs.

6. **Promote Your Content**: Share your content on social media platforms, relevant online communities, and industry forums. Engage with your audience by responding to comments and encouraging discussions around your content.

7. **Implement Email Marketing Campaigns**: Use an email marketing platform to design and send targeted email campaigns. Personalize your emails based on the segmented lists you created earlier. Include engaging content, special offers, and calls to action to drive conversions.

8. **Track and Analyze Results**: Regularly monitor the performance of your email marketing and content marketing

efforts. Track metrics like open rates, click-through rates, and conversions. Use this data to refine your strategies and improve future campaigns.

9. **Continuously Provide Value**: Consistently deliver valuable content to your audience through email newsletters, blog posts, or other channels. Keep your subscribers engaged by offering exclusive content, discounts, or early access to new products or services.

10. **Build Relationships**: Engage with your audience by responding to their emails or comments, addressing their concerns, and providing helpful information. Building strong customer relationships fosters loyalty and encourages them to become brand advocates.

11. **Stay Compliant**: Familiarize yourself with regulations like the General Data Protection Regulation (GDPR) and the Controlling the Assault of Non-Solicited Pornography And Marketing (CAN-SPAM) Act. Ensure that you have proper consent from individuals before sending marketing emails and provide easy options for unsubscribing.

12. **Stay Updated**: Keep up with the latest trends and best practices in email and content marketing. Attend webinars, read industry blogs, and participate in relevant communities to stay informed and continue learning.

By incorporating email marketing and content marketing into your business strategy, you can effectively reach and engage your target audience, build brand authority, and drive business growth in the Indian market.

Case Study: How Company X Leveraged Email and Content Marketing for Business Growth

Background Company X, a leading e-commerce platform in the fashion industry, was looking to enhance its digital marketing efforts to drive customer engagement, increase brand loyalty, and boost sales. They implemented a comprehensive strategy incorporating email and content marketing to achieve their goals.

Approach

1. **Building a Robust Email List**: Company X implemented various strategies to build a quality email list. They placed prominent email subscription forms on their website and offered exclusive discounts to incentivize sign-ups. They also leveraged social media advertising campaigns to attract potential customers to subscribe to their newsletter.

2. **Segmentation and Personalization**: Company X utilized customer data to segment their email list based on demographics, purchase history, and browsing behavior. This allowed them to create highly targeted email campaigns that provided personalized recommendations, relevant product updates, and exclusive offers tailored to each customer segment.

3. **Compelling Content Creation**: The company engaged its audience with practical and relevant content. They regularly published blog posts, how-to guides, and fashion trend articles that appealed to their target audience. They also produced high-quality visuals, such as lookbooks and style inspiration images, to captivate their customers.

4. **Email Campaigns**: Company X implemented a series of email campaigns to nurture leads, promote new products, and drive sales. They used automated drip campaigns to onboard new subscribers and guide them through the customer journey. They also sent personalized product recommendations based on customers' browsing and purchase history.

5. **Integration of Email and Content**: The company strategically integrated its content marketing efforts with email marketing campaigns. They featured blog post summaries and exclusive content previews in their emails, driving traffic to their website and increasing engagement. They also included social sharing buttons in their emails to encourage subscribers to share the content with their networks.

6. **Measurement and Optimization**: Company X regularly measured the performance of their email and content marketing efforts. They analyzed vital metrics such as open rates, click-through rates, conversion rates, and revenue generated from email campaigns. Based on these insights, they continuously optimized their strategies and tested different subject lines, content formats, and CTAs to improve engagement and conversion rates.

Results

By implementing a comprehensive email and content marketing strategy, Company X achieved remarkable results:

- **Increased Customer Engagement**: The personalized and relevant content delivered through email campaigns resulted in higher open and click-through rates. Customers felt more connected to the brand, leading to increased engagement with their website and social media channels.

- **Enhanced Brand Loyalty**: By consistently delivering valuable content and personalized recommendations, Company X fostered a sense of loyalty among their customers. Repeat purchases and customer referrals increased, contributing to a growing customer base.
- **Revenue Growth**: The combination of targeted email campaigns and compelling content increased sales and revenue for Company X. Customers were likelier to purchase based on the personalized product recommendations and exclusive offers they received through email.
- **Improved Customer Satisfaction**: The valuable content provided by Company X helped customers make informed purchasing decisions. This led to higher customer satisfaction levels and a reduction in product returns.
- **Positive Brand Perception**: Through their content marketing efforts, Company X positioned itself as a trusted authority in the fashion industry. Customers perceived the brand as reliable, knowledgeable, and dedicated to providing value beyond just selling products.

Conclusion

By leveraging the power of email marketing and content marketing, Company X successfully enhanced customer engagement built brand loyalty, and achieved significant revenue growth. The strategic integration of personalized email campaigns and compelling content creation allowed them to connect with their audience deeper, driving sales and fostering a positive brand perception. This case study demonstrates the immense potential of combining email and content marketing to drive business growth and establish a strong brand presence in the competitive e-commerce industry.

The power of analytics and understanding consumer behavior

In the expansive field of digital marketing, a crucial tool remains essential across strategies: analytics. By comprehending analytics and interpreting consumer behavior, businesses can make informed decisions based on data, refine processes, and establish a stronger connection with their audience. Let's delve into this captivating interplay of numbers, patterns, and consumer insights.

1. Analytics: The Crucial Component of Effective Digital Strategies

In today's digital landscape, analytics is pivotal in shaping successful strategies. It involves collecting, analyzing, and interpreting data about user interactions with digital assets, providing valuable insights for decision-making.

- **What is Analytics?** Analytics refers to tools and techniques used to measure, process, and interpret data related to user interactions with digital assets. Businesses can better understand user behavior and optimize their digital presence by leveraging analytics.
- **Metrics Matter:** When evaluating the effectiveness of digital strategies, metrics are of utmost importance. Page views,

bounce rates, and conversion rates are just a few metrics that provide valuable insights into user engagement and conversion. By focusing on the right metrics that align with your objectives, you can make informed decisions and drive meaningful results.

2. Decoding Consumer Behavior

Understanding consumer behavior is crucial for businesses to effectively engage with their target audience. Several strategies can be employed to gain insights into consumer behavior and enhance their experience with your brand.

- **Journey Mapping**: By meticulously tracking the consumer's path through your digital assets, you can comprehensively understand their interactions. This includes identifying touchpoints where they engage with your brand, drop-off points where they lose interest, and valuable opportunities for further engagement.
- **Intent Indicators**: To tailor content and advertisements to meet the specific needs of consumers, it is essential to decipher their intent. You can gain valuable insights into their preferences and intentions by analyzing their searches, clicks, and dwell time on your digital platforms.
- **Feedback and Surveys**: While quantitative data from analytics can provide valuable insights into consumer behavior, gathering direct consumer feedback is equally important. Feedback and surveys allow businesses to capture qualitative insights and better understand consumer preferences, opinions, and satisfaction levels.

By employing these strategies, businesses can understand consumer behavior comprehensively and make informed decisions to optimize their marketing efforts and enhance the overall consumer experience.

3. Personalization Through Insights

- **Tailored Experiences**: By leveraging deep insights into user behavior and preferences, we can create highly customized experiences that truly resonate with each user. This level of personalization not only enhances user engagement but also fosters a stronger connection between the user and our brand.
- **Dynamic Content**: By harnessing the power of advanced analytics, we can serve dynamic content that adapts in real time to our users' changing needs and interests. This ensures they always receive the most relevant and up-to-date information, providing a more satisfying and valuable user experience.

4. Predictive Analysis: Anticipating Future Trends

Predictive analysis is crucial in helping businesses stay ahead of the curve. By leveraging advanced analytics tools such as machine learning and AI, companies can gain valuable insights into future trends based on past behavior. This enables them to make informed decisions and take proactive measures to capitalize on emerging opportunities.

One key aspect of predictive analysis is consumer lifecycle predictions. By understanding the different stages of a consumer's lifecycle, businesses can anticipate their needs and preferences at each location. This allows them to offer tailored solutions and targeted, relevant, timely, and timely offers. By effectively predicting consumer behavior, businesses can enhance customer satisfaction, drive customer loyalty, and ultimately achieve business growth.

In summary, predictive analysis empowers businesses to make accurate forecasts and predictions, enabling them to stay ahead of the competition and meet the evolving needs of their customers.

5. Real-Time Decision Making

In today's fast-paced business environment, real-time decision-making has become crucial for businesses to stay competitive and adapt to changing market conditions. Here are a few critical aspects of real-time decision-making:

- **Real-Time Data**: With the advancements in analytics tools, businesses can now access and analyze real-time data. This means that decision-makers can make informed choices based on up-to-the-minute information. By monitoring real-time data, companies can identify trends, spot opportunities, and address any issues promptly. This enables them to adjust their strategies and immediately stay ahead of the competition.
- **A/B Testing**: Another essential aspect of real-time decision-making is A/B testing. This method allows businesses to simultaneously test two versions of a webpage, ad, or campaign and compare their performance. By analyzing the results in real time, companies can gain valuable insights into what works and what doesn't. This iterative process of refining and optimizing in real-time helps companies improve their marketing efforts, enhance customer experiences, and ultimately drive better results.

Real-time decision-making empowers businesses to be agile and responsive, ensuring they make data-driven choices and maximize their chances of success in a rapidly evolving business landscape.

6. Challenges in Analytics and Behavior Analysis

- **Data Overload**: With the ever-increasing volume of data generated, organizations often face the challenge of dealing with data overload. It becomes crucial to effectively filter out noise and extract meaningful insights to drive actionable strategies.
- **Privacy Concerns**: In today's data-driven world, privacy concerns loom large. With regulations like GDPR (General Data Protection Regulation), organizations must prioritize data collection and processing methods that adhere to strict privacy standards. This ensures the protection of individuals' personal information while still leveraging data for analysis and behavior insights.
- **Interpreting Data Correctly**: The interpretation of data plays a vital role in shaping effective strategies. Misinterpretation or misrepresentation of data can lead to better decision-making processes. Investing time and effort in thoroughly understanding the data or seeking expert guidance is essential to avoid making faulty assumptions or drawing incorrect conclusions.

7. Continuous Learning, Staying Updated, and Expanding Knowledge

To thrive in the ever-evolving world of analytics, it is crucial to continuously update your skills and knowledge. Here are some ways to achieve this:

- **Stay Up-to-Date with Emerging Tools**: The analytics field constantly advances, with new tools and methodologies developed regularly. It is essential to stay informed about the latest advancements and incorporate them into your work.

- **Monitor Consumer Behavior Shifts**: Consumer preferences and behaviors are not static, and they can change over time. Regularly analyzing market trends and consumer data ensures that your strategies and approaches remain relevant and practical.

- **Invest in Training and Workshops**: Enhancing your team's skills is essential for maximizing the potential of analytics. Consider investing in training programs and workshops on the latest analytics tools and techniques. This will enable your team to stay ahead of the curve and maximize the available resources.

Remember, continuous learning and staying updated are crucial to analytics success. By embracing new knowledge and adapting to changing consumer behaviors, you can ensure that your strategies and analytics efforts are always practical and impactful.

8. Expanding the Scope of Analytics

- **Unveiling the Narrative in Data**: Rather than merely examining numbers, delve into the stories they reveal about user journeys, preferences, and pain points, gaining deeper insights.

- **Comprehensive Perspective**: Combine analytics from multiple channels to obtain a comprehensive view of consumer behavior, guaranteeing that no valuable insights go unnoticed. Additionally, this approach allows for a more thorough understanding of the consumer landscape.

Conclusion

Analytics is not just a backdrop but a central player in shaping digital strategies. By leveraging the wealth of data and comprehending the underlying patterns of consumer behavior, businesses can establish meaningful connections, anticipate needs, and continuously refine their approach for maximum impact.

Walkthrough: How an Indian SMB Can Use the Power of Analytics and Consumer Behavior to Grow Their Business

1. **Define Business Objectives**: Start by clearly defining your business objectives. Are you looking to increase sales, improve customer satisfaction, or expand your market reach? Understanding your goals will help you align your analytics efforts.

2. **Collect and Analyze Data**: Implement tracking mechanisms to collect relevant data from your website, social media channels, and other digital platforms. Use analytics tools like Google Analytics to analyze user behavior, website traffic, and engagement metrics.

3. **Segment Your Audience**: Divide your customer base into segments based on demographics, buying behavior, and preferences. This segmentation will help you understand your customers better and tailor your marketing strategies accordingly.

4. **Identify Key Metrics**: Determine the key metrics that align with your business objectives. For example, track conversion rates, average order value, customer lifetime value, and customer retention rate. These metrics will provide insights into the effectiveness of your marketing efforts and customer satisfaction.

5. **Analyze Consumer Behavior**: Use analytics tools to gain insights into consumer behavior. Monitor website navigation patterns, time spent on different pages, and click-through rates. Identify trends, such as popular products or pages, and optimize your marketing strategies based on these insights.

6. **Personalization and Targeting**: Leverage consumer behavior insights to personalize your marketing campaigns. Use targeted email marketing, personalized recommendations, and customized offers to enhance the customer experience and drive conversions.

7. **Optimize Marketing Channels**: Analyze the performance of your marketing channels, such as social media, search engine marketing, and email marketing. Identify which channels are driving the most engagement and conversions. Allocate your budget accordingly to maximize ROI.

8. **Continuous Monitoring and Optimization**: Regularly monitor your analytics data and make data-driven decisions. Identify areas for improvement and implement A/B testing to optimize your marketing campaigns. Continuously refine your strategies based on consumer behavior insights.

9. **Customer Feedback and Surveys**: Actively seek customer feedback through surveys, reviews, and social media interactions. Use this feedback to understand customer preferences, pain points, and areas for improvement. Incorporate these insights into your business strategies and product development.

10. **Stay Updated with Industry Trends**: Keep abreast of industry trends, emerging technologies, and consumer behavior shifts. Attend industry conferences, webinars, and workshops to expand your knowledge and stay ahead of the competition.

11. **Measure and Track Results**: Regularly measure and track the results of your analytics efforts. Assess the impact of your strategies on critical metrics like sales, customer satisfaction, and market share. Use these insights to refine your approach and drive business growth.

By harnessing the power of analytics and consumer behavior insights, Indian SMBs can make informed business decisions, optimize their marketing efforts, and enhance the overall customer experience. Remember to tailor your strategies to your business needs and adapt to changing consumer behavior.

Case Study: How Analytics Transformed a Retail Business

Business Background: ABC Retail is a well-established brick-and-mortar retailer with multiple stores nationwide. The company faced challenges understanding customer behavior, optimizing inventory management, and enhancing the shopping experience. ABC Retail leveraged analytics and consumer behavior insights to overcome these challenges.

Approach: ABC Retail implemented a comprehensive analytics solution to collect and analyze data from various sources, including point-of-sale systems, loyalty programs, and online interactions. The goal was to understand customer preferences better, optimize inventory, and personalize the shopping experience.

Key Findings and Strategies:

1. **Customer Segmentation:** Through data analysis, ABC Retail discovered that its customer base could be segmented into different groups based on demographics, shopping patterns,

and preferences. This allowed them to tailor marketing campaigns and promotions to specific customer segments, increasing engagement and sales.

2. **Inventory Optimization:** By analyzing purchasing patterns and seasonality trends, ABC Retail gained insights into which products were in high demand and when. Leveraging this information, they optimized their inventory management processes, ensuring that popular items were always in stock and reducing excess inventory costs.

3. **Personalized Recommendations:** ABC Retail implemented a recommendation engine on its website and in-store displays using customer browsing and purchase history data. This engine provided customized product recommendations to customers, increasing cross-selling and upselling opportunities.

4. **In-Store Experience Enhancement:** With analytics, ABC Retail identified areas for improvement in their physical stores. They analyzed foot traffic patterns, customer flow, and product placement to optimize store layouts and improve the shopping experience. This led to increased customer satisfaction and repeat visits.

Results: The implementation of analytics and consumer behavior insights had a significant impact on ABC Retail's business:

- **Revenue Growth:** By tailoring marketing efforts and improving inventory management, ABC Retail experienced a steady increase in revenue. Personalized recommendations and targeted promotions drove higher conversion rates and average transaction values.

- **Improved Customer Satisfaction:** The enhanced shopping experience, personalized recommendations, and optimized store layouts improved customer satisfaction and loyalty. Customer feedback indicated higher levels of engagement and a deepened connection with the brand.

- **Operational Efficiency:** Using analytics allowed ABC Retail to streamline its inventory management processes, reducing costs associated with overstocking and stockouts. This led to improved operational efficiency and increased profitability.

Conclusion: The case study of ABC Retail demonstrates the transformative power of analytics and consumer behavior insights in a retail business. By leveraging these insights, companies can optimize marketing efforts, improve inventory management, enhance the overall customer experience, and drive revenue growth. As more businesses embrace analytics, the competitive advantage gained through data-driven decision-making becomes indispensable in today's retail landscape.

THE E-COMMERCE BOOM

Choosing the right platform

When venturing into the world of e-commerce, one of the most critical decisions you'll have to make is selecting the perfect platform for your online store. The platform you choose will serve as the very foundation of your business, playing a vital role in determining its functionality, user experience, and potential for growth and expansion. In this chapter, we will thoroughly explore the vast array of options available to you and carefully consider all the essential factors to consider when making this pivotal decision. By the end of this chapter, you will be equipped with the knowledge and insights necessary to confidently choose the ideal e-commerce platform that perfectly aligns with your business's unique needs and goals.

1. Identifying Your Business Requirements

Several key factors must be considered when selecting the right platform for your business. These factors will help you determine which platform best suits your needs and aligns with your long-term goals. Let's dive into these factors in more detail:

- **Size of Your Business:** The size of your business plays a crucial role in choosing the right platform. Whether you're a small boutique or a large enterprise, some platforms cater specifically to your business size.
- **Product Complexity:** Another important consideration is the complexity of your product. Different platforms are designed to

handle various digital, physical, subscription-based, or combination products. Understanding the nature of your product will guide you in selecting the most suitable platform.

- **Customization and Scalability**: Looking ahead to the future, it's essential to consider your long-term goals. Do you anticipate the need for extensive customization options to tailor the platform to your specific requirements? Or do you expect rapid growth and scalability, requiring a platform that can easily handle increased demand? Evaluating your customization and scalability needs will ensure that you choose a platform that can adapt and grow with your business.

By carefully assessing these factors and understanding your unique business requirements, you will be well-equipped to decide when to select a platform that best supports your business needs.

2. Key E-commerce Platform Features

- **User-Friendly Interface**: A straightforward admin interface ensures smooth store management without a steep learning curve. Additionally, the platform can provide customizable templates and drag-and-drop functionality, allowing users to easily design their store according to their preferences.
- **Mobile Optimization**: With the rise of e-commerce, platforms must offer mobile-responsive store designs. This includes mobile-friendly layouts, optimized checkout processes for mobile devices, and the ability to integrate with mobile payment methods seamlessly.
- **Payment Gateways**: Ensure the platform supports various secure payment methods. This includes popular options like credit cards, digital wallets, and cryptocurrency. Additionally,

the platform should have built-in fraud detection and prevention measures to ensure secure transactions.

- **SEO Capabilities**: Built-in SEO tools can aid in driving organic traffic to your store. These tools can include features like meta tag customization, URL optimization, sitemap generation, and integration with popular search engines. Moreover, the platform can provide analytics and reporting features to help monitor and improve the store's search engine rankings.

3. Understanding the Giants: Shopify, WooCommerce, Magento, and More

- **Shopify**: Known for its user-friendliness, Shopify is a hosted solution ideal for startups and small businesses. With its intuitive interface and extensive app marketplace, Shopify provides a seamless experience for entrepreneurs looking to establish their online presence.
- **WooCommerce**: A powerful WordPress plugin offering a high degree of customization. Suitable for those familiar with WordPress, WooCommerce allows users to create tailored online stores that align with their unique branding and design preferences. With its vast array of themes and plugins, WooCommerce provides endless possibilities for making an impressive online shopping experience.
- **Magento**: Catering to medium to large enterprises, Magento is a robust platform renowned for its scalability and customization options. With its extensive feature set and advanced functionalities, Magento empowers businesses to build and manage complex online stores that can handle high volumes of traffic and transactions. Whether managing multiple storefronts or implementing advanced marketing

strategies, Magento offers the flexibility and tools to meet the demands of ambitious e-commerce ventures.

- **Others**: Besides these giants, other noteworthy platforms offer unique advantages and should be considered based on specific needs. For instance, BigCommerce is known for its seamless integration with popular marketplaces like Amazon and eBay, making it an excellent choice for businesses looking to expand their reach. On the other hand, Wix offers a user-friendly website builder with drag-and-drop functionality, making it an ideal option for those who prioritize ease of use. Lastly, Squarespace stands out for its stunning templates and design-focused approach, making it an excellent choice for businesses that value aesthetics and visual appeal.

When choosing an e-commerce platform, it's essential to carefully evaluate each option's features, scalability, customization options, and pricing plans. By understanding the strengths and weaknesses of these giants and considering other alternatives, you can make an informed decision that aligns with your business goals and requirements.

4. Self-hosted vs. Hosted Solutions

When choosing a platform for your business, you have two main options: self-hosted and hosted solutions. Let's look at each option to help you make an informed decision.

- **Self-hosted Platforms**: Self-hosted platforms offer you greater control and customization over your website or application. With a self-hosted solution, you can choose your hosting provider, ensuring that your website is hosted in a way that suits your needs. Additionally, self-hosted platforms allow you complete control over your website's security measures and updates. This means you can implement the security protocols necessary and ensure that your website is constantly updated with the latest features and improvements.

- **Hosted Solutions**: On the other hand, if you prefer a more hassle-free approach, hosted solutions might be the right choice. Hosted solutions are 'out-of-the-box' platforms where the provider takes care of hosting. This means you don't have to worry about finding a hosting provider, setting up servers, or managing security measures. Hosted solutions often come with pre-built templates and features, making it easier to get started quickly. While customization options might be more limited compared to self-hosted platforms, hosted solutions still offer a range of customization features to ensure your website reflects your brand identity.

Choosing between self-hosted platforms and hosted solutions depends on your needs and preferences. A self-hosted platform best fits you if you value complete control and customization and have the resources to handle hosting and updates. However, if you prefer a more convenient and hassle-free option and don't require extensive customization, a hosted solution could be the way to go. Consider your business goals, technical expertise, and budget when deciding.

5. Budget Considerations

When considering the budget for your online platform, it's essential to consider various factors that can contribute to the overall costs. Here are some key points to consider:

- **Setup Costs:** It's worth noting that some platforms may require initial setup fees or the purchase of themes to customize your website according to your preferences.

- **Monthly Fees:** Besides the initial setup costs, many hosted solutions come with monthly or annual subscription fees. These fees cover the platform's hosting services, maintenance, and support.
- **Transaction Fees:** It's essential to know that specific platforms may charge a fee per transaction, mainly if you use their integrated payment gateways. These fees are typically a tiny percentage of each transaction and can vary depending on the platform.
- **Additional Costs:** Apart from the costs above, it's also crucial to consider any other expenses that may arise. This includes costs for plugins or extensions that enhance the functionality of your platform, as well as potential future custom development if you decide to customize your online presence further.

By considering these various budget considerations, you can ensure that you have a comprehensive understanding of the costs involved in setting up and maintaining your online platform.

6. Community and Support

- **Vibrant Community:** Platforms with active communities can benefit users by providing a rich ecosystem to seek help, share experiences, troubleshoot issues, and discover new plugins and tools to enhance their experience.
- **Official Support:** It is essential to prioritize platforms that offer robust official support. This ensures that users can access reliable assistance whenever they encounter technical difficulties, have queries, or require guidance. Prompt and dedicated support from the platform's team can significantly enhance the user experience and provide peace of mind.

7. Flexibility and Integration

- **Extensions, Plugins, and Integrations**: One of the critical advantages of a robust e-commerce platform is its ability to integrate seamlessly with other tools and services. By offering a wide range of extensions and plugins, the platform allows you to enhance your store's functionality and connect it with various third-party solutions, such as CRMs, email marketing tools, and inventory management systems.
- **API Access and Customization**: Another essential aspect to consider is the availability of API access. Access to the platform's API allows for advanced customization and integration capabilities, enabling you to tailor your online store to meet your unique business needs. With API access, you can create custom features, automate processes, and integrate with other systems, ultimately providing your customers a more personalized and efficient shopping experience.

8. Future-Proofing Your Store

To future-proof your store and ensure its long-term success, there are a few key considerations to keep in mind:

- **Scalability**: Choosing a platform that can scale along with your business is crucial. As your business grows, you will inevitably need to add more products, handle increased website traffic, and process more transactions. By selecting a platform that can handle these growing demands without any hiccups, you can ensure a seamless and uninterrupted shopping experience for your customers.
- **Updates and Trends**: In the rapidly evolving world of e-commerce, staying ahead of the curve is essential. Choosing a

platform that regularly updates and adapts to the latest e-commerce trends will keep your store looking fresh and contemporary and ensure your website's security. Regular updates help patch any vulnerabilities and protect against potential security threats, giving you peace of mind knowing that your customer's information is safe.

By considering these factors and selecting a platform that offers scalability and keeps up with updates and trends, you can future-proof your store and position it for long-term success in the ever-changing world of e-commerce.

9. Making the Transition

For those who are considering switching platforms, it is essential to take the following factors into account:

- **Data Migration**: One crucial aspect is ensuring the new platform supports seamless data transfer. This includes not only the transfer of products but also the transfer of customer data and order histories. It is essential to have a smooth transition without any loss or distortion of data.
- **SEO Preservation**: Another essential consideration when migrating platforms is the potential impact on SEO rankings. Implementing proper redirects and retaining URL structures is crucial to preserve the SEO efforts made. By doing so, you can maintain the visibility and rankings achieved, ensuring a seamless transition without negatively impacting your website's search engine performance.

Conclusion

Choosing the right e-commerce platform is not a decision to be taken lightly. It sets the stage for your online business journey. By considering your unique business needs, budget, and desired features and investing time in research, you can select a platform that serves your current requirements and supports your future aspirations.

Walkthrough

Here is a step-by-step walkthrough for an Indian SMB (Small and Medium-sized Business) to implement an e-commerce platform into their business:

1. **Identify Your Business Requirements**: Assess your business's size, product complexity, customization needs, and scalability requirements. This will help you determine which e-commerce platform best suits your needs.
2. **Choose the Right Platform**: Consider popular e-commerce platforms like Shopify, WooCommerce, and Magento. Research their features, scalability options, customization capabilities, and pricing plans to find the platform that aligns with your business goals.
3. **Setup and Customization**: Once you've selected a platform, sign up and follow the setup instructions provided by the platform. Customize your online store by choosing an appropriate theme, adding branding elements, and configuring the store settings.
4. **Product Listing and Inventory Management**: Add your products to the platform, including images, descriptions, and pricing. Implement inventory management tools to track and manage your stock effectively.

5. **Payment Gateway Integration:** Choose a payment gateway that caters to the Indian market and integrates with your chosen platform. Ensure that it supports popular payment methods in India, such as credit/debit cards, net banking, and mobile wallets.

6. **Shipping and Logistics:** Set up shipping methods and configure shipping rates based on your business's requirements. Integrate with reliable logistics partners to ensure smooth order fulfillment and timely delivery.

7. **Localized Content and Language:** Customize your online store to cater to the Indian market by providing localized content, including product descriptions, pricing in Indian Rupees (INR), and customer support in regional languages if feasible.

8. **Marketing and Promotion:** Implement digital marketing strategies to drive traffic to your online store. Utilize social media marketing, search engine optimization (SEO), and email marketing to reach your target audience and promote your products effectively.

9. **Customer Support:** Offer multiple channels for customer support, such as email, chat, and phone. Ensure prompt and efficient customer service to build customer trust and loyalty.

10. **Analytics and Reporting:** Utilize the analytics and reporting features provided by your chosen platform to track key metrics, such as website traffic, conversion rates, and sales. Use this data to make informed business decisions and optimize your online store's performance.

11. **Security and Data Protection:** Implement robust security measures to protect customer data and ensure secure transactions. Utilize SSL certificates, secure payment gateways,

and regular software updates to safeguard your online store and customer information.

12. **Continuous Improvement**: Regularly evaluate your online store's performance and make necessary improvements based on customer feedback and market trends. Stay updated with the latest e-commerce trends and technologies to remain competitive in the Indian market.

By following these steps and continuously refining your online store, you can successfully implement an e-commerce platform into your Indian SMB and leverage the immense potential of online selling in the Indian market.

Case Study: Transforming a Traditional Brick-and-Mortar Business into a Successful E-commerce Store

Background

The client, a family-owned retail business with multiple physical stores, wanted to expand its reach and tap into the growing online market. They approached our team to help them transition their business into a thriving e-commerce store while preserving their brand identity and customer base.

Challenges

- Limited online presence: The client needed more e-commerce experience, knowledge, and resources to establish an online store.
- Competing with established online retailers: The client faced fierce competition from well-established online retailers in

their industry, making it crucial to differentiate and provide unique value to customers.

- Inventory management: The client needed an efficient system to manage their extensive inventory across multiple locations, ensuring accurate stock availability and timely order fulfillment.
- Seamless customer experience: The client wanted to replicate their personalized and attentive customer experience in their physical stores, ensuring a smooth transition to an online platform.

Strategy and Implementation

1. **Platform Selection**: After thoroughly analyzing the client's requirements, budget, and growth aspirations, we recommended the client choose Shopify as their e-commerce platform. Shopify offers a user-friendly interface, a wide range of customizable themes, and robust inventory management capabilities.

2. **Design and Branding**: We worked closely with the client to design an online store that reflected their brand identity and provided a seamless customer experience. Customizable Shopify themes were tailored to match the client's existing branding elements and create a cohesive online presence.

3. **Product Listing and Inventory Management**: We implemented Shopify's inventory management system, allowing clients to manage their stock across multiple locations efficiently. Automated syncing ensured real-time inventory updates, preventing overselling and improving order fulfillment.

4. **Payment Gateway Integration**: To provide a secure and convenient payment experience, we integrated popular payment gateways, including credit cards, digital wallets, and cash on delivery. This allowed customers to choose their preferred payment method, boosting trust and conversion rates.

5. **Order Fulfillment and Logistics**: We partnered with reliable logistics providers to streamline order fulfillment and ensure timely delivery. Integration with shipping carriers enabled real-time shipping rate calculation and tracking, enhancing the customer experience.

6. **Customer Engagement**: To replicate the personalized in-store experience, we implemented live chat support and integrated a customer relationship management (CRM) system. This allowed the client to provide real-time assistance, track customer interactions, and nurture long-term customer relationships.

7. **Digital Marketing and Promotion**: We developed a comprehensive digital marketing strategy, including search engine optimization (SEO), social media, and email marketing. Targeted campaigns and engaging content helped drive traffic to the client's online store and increase brand visibility.

8. **Analytics and Reporting**: We set up tools to track key performance metrics, such as website traffic, conversion rates, and sales. Regular reporting and analysis provided valuable insights to optimize marketing efforts, identify trends, and make data-driven decisions.

Results and Benefits

- Increased revenue: The client experienced significant revenue growth after launching their e-commerce store, expanding their customer reach beyond their physical store locations.
- Improved customer experience: Customers appreciated the convenience of online shopping while still receiving personalized support and attention through live chat and CRM integration.
- Streamlined operations: The client's inventory management and order fulfillment processes became more efficient, reducing errors and improving overall operational productivity.
- Enhanced brand visibility: Through effective digital marketing strategies, the client's brand gained recognition and attracted a wider audience, increasing brand awareness and customer engagement.
- Scalability and growth: The chosen e-commerce platform provided the scalability required to accommodate the client's future growth plans, allowing them to expand their product offerings and explore new markets.

Conclusion

By leveraging the power of e-commerce and implementing a comprehensive strategy, our team successfully transformed the client's traditional brick-and-mortar business into a thriving online store. The client experienced significant growth, improved customer engagement, and streamlined operations, positioning them for long-term success in the digital landscape.

Enhancing the user experience

The quality of products does not solely determine the success of an e-commerce website. While product quality is essential, focusing on the overall user experience (UX) is equally crucial. A seamless, intuitive, and engaging UX can significantly impact the success of an e-commerce website. It can make the difference between a completed sale and an abandoned cart.

In this chapter, we will delve into various strategies and elements that are crucial in crafting an optimal e-commerce user experience. By implementing these strategies and incorporating these elements, you can enhance the overall user experience and increase the chances of converting visitors into loyal customers. It is essential to consider factors such as website navigation, visual design, user interface, and customer engagement techniques. By paying attention to these aspects, you can create a user-friendly and enjoyable shopping experience for your customers.

1. Importance of First Impressions

When it comes to attracting and retaining customers, first impressions are crucial. Here are some key factors to consider:

- **Website Load Time:** Ensuring your website loads quickly is of utmost importance. Studies have shown that even a few seconds of delay in loading time can significantly increase the chances of potential customers abandoning your site.

Therefore, optimizing your website's load time is essential to provide a seamless browsing experience for your visitors.

- **Clean Design**: A visually appealing and uncluttered design is vital in creating a positive first impression. A well-designed website with a clean layout catches users' attention and enhances their overall browsing experience. By incorporating a clean design, you can make it easier for visitors to navigate through your site and find the information they are looking for.

Remember, first impressions can determine whether a visitor chooses to stay on your website or leave, so it is crucial to prioritize these elements to make a lasting impact on your audience.

2. Product Presentation

- **High-Quality Images**: It is essential to provide not just one but multiple high-quality images for each product. These images should be zoomable, allowing users to examine the details of the product closely. By offering a variety of prints, customers can get a comprehensive view of the product from different angles.
- **Detailed Descriptions**: Besides high-quality images, providing precise descriptions for each product is crucial. These descriptions should be clear, concise, and informative, answering potential customer queries. Customers can make informed purchasing decisions by providing comprehensive details about the product's features, specifications, and benefits.
- **Video Demonstrations**: Another effective way to enhance the product presentation is by including video demonstrations. These videos can showcase the product, providing additional

clarity and confidence to potential buyers. Customers can better understand its functionality and value by visually demonstrating how the product works and highlighting its key features.

A successful product presentation should include high-quality images, detailed descriptions, and video demonstrations. By implementing these strategies, businesses can effectively convey the value and benefits of their products to potential customers, ultimately increasing sales and customer satisfaction.

3. Enhancing Navigational Ease

- **Precise Categorization**: By organizing products into logical and clear categories and subcategories, users can effortlessly locate the items they are looking for in a shorter amount of time.
- **Effective Search**: To facilitate a seamless user experience, it is crucial to incorporate a robust search function that provides accurate results and auto-suggestions and filters. This will enable users to refine their search queries and narrow their options more efficiently.
- **Breadcrumb Navigation**: Implementing a breadcrumb navigation system will significantly enhance the user's understanding of their navigation path within the website. This feature allows users to quickly backtrack and retrace their steps, making navigating different sections and pages more straightforward.
- **Visual Indicators**: Another effective way to improve navigational ease is by incorporating visual indicators such as icons or color-coded labels. These visual cues can help users

quickly identify different sections or categories, making navigating and locating the desired products easier.

- **User-Friendly Menu**: Creating a user-friendly menu that is intuitive and easy to navigate is essential for enhancing navigational ease. This can be achieved by using clear and concise labels, organizing menu items logically, and ensuring that the menu is easily accessible from any page on the website.

- **Related Product Recommendations**: Including related product recommendations based on user browsing history or previous purchases can also contribute to a longer and more engaging user experience. By suggesting relevant products, users are encouraged to explore more options and potentially make additional purchases.

- **Interactive Filters**: Incorporating interactive filters that allow users to refine their search results based on specific criteria (e.g., price range, color, size) can significantly enhance their ability to find exactly what they want. This feature gives users more control over their search and helps them discover products tailored to their preferences.

4. Mobile Optimization

- **Responsive Design**: It is crucial to ensure that the website is designed to adapt seamlessly across various devices, with particular attention given to mobile devices. As the popularity of m-commerce continues to grow, businesses need to provide a user-friendly experience on mobile platforms.

- **Touch-Friendly**: To enhance the user experience on mobile devices, it is essential to ensure that buttons and clickable elements are correctly sized and spaced to facilitate easy touch navigation. By optimizing the touch-friendliness of the website, businesses can ensure that users can effortlessly interact with the content and functionalities on their mobile devices.

5. Enhancing the Checkout Experience

- **Simplified Process**: Make the checkout process more efficient and user-friendly, eliminating unnecessary steps and minimizing the time needed to purchase.
- **Guest-Friendly Checkout**: Provide the option for users to proceed with the checkout process without creating an account, ensuring a hassle-free experience.
- **Transparent and Comprehensive Pricing**: Ensure that all costs, including shipping fees and taxes, are presented to customers from the beginning, avoiding any surprises at the final stage of the purchase.
- **Seamless Payment Options**: Offer a variety of secure and convenient payment methods to cater to customers' diverse preferences and needs.
- **Personalized Recommendations**: Implement a recommendation engine that suggests relevant products or complementary items during checkout, enhancing the overall shopping experience and potentially increasing the average order value.

6. Building Trust

To build trust with your customers, it is essential to consider the following trust indicators:

- **Secure Transactions**: One way to assure users of safe transactions is by implementing SSL certificates and prominently displaying security badges on your website. This will give users confidence that their personal and financial information is protected.

- **Reviews and Testimonials**: Displaying genuine customer reviews and testimonials can significantly build trust. Positive feedback from satisfied customers serves as social proof and reassures potential customers about the quality and reliability of your products or services.

- **Clear Return and Refund Policies**: Communicating your return and refund policies is crucial in fostering trust. Ensure that users understand the purchase terms, including the process for returning or refunding products. This transparency will create a sense of security and confidence in potential customers.

Building customer trust is essential for establishing long-lasting relationships and driving sales. By implementing these trust indicators, you can instill confidence in your customers and differentiate yourself from competitors.

7. Interactive Elements

- **Live Chat**: Provide a live chat feature on your website or app to offer immediate assistance to users. This will allow them to ask questions, seek guidance, and get real-time support for queries or concerns. A live chat option can significantly enhance the user experience and improve customer satisfaction.

- **Personalized Recommendations**: Utilize advanced algorithms and machine learning techniques to analyze user browsing history and behavior. This data allows you to generate customized product recommendations for each user. These recommendations can be displayed prominently on your website or app, enticing users to explore and discover new products that align with their interests and preferences. By offering personalized recommendations, you can increase user engagement, encourage repeat visits, and drive more conversions.

8. Enhancing Accessibility for All

- **Design for Individuals with Disabilities**: It is essential to prioritize the website's usability for individuals with disabilities. This can be achieved by carefully considering factors such as color contrasts, font sizes, and compatibility with screen readers. By implementing these design considerations, we can ensure that users with disabilities have equal access to the website's content and functionalities.
- **Expanding Language and Currency Options**: To reach a wider global audience, providing language and currency options on the website is crucial. Users from different linguistic backgrounds can easily navigate and understand the content by offering multiple language choices. Additionally, incorporating currency options allows users to view prices and make transactions in their preferred currency, enhancing their overall experience and increasing the likelihood of conversions.

9. Feedback and Continuous Improvement

- **User Feedback**: Actively solicit user feedback through surveys, interviews, and user testing sessions to gain valuable insights into their experiences, pain points, and suggestions for improvement. This feedback will help identify areas needing attention and guide continuous improvement.
- **Analytics**: Utilize powerful tools such as Google Analytics to gather comprehensive data on user behavior, website traffic,

bounce rates, conversion funnels, and other vital metrics. By analyzing this data, we can better understand how users interact with our platform and identify specific areas for optimization and enhancement. This data-driven approach enables us to make informed decisions and implement targeted improvements to enhance the user experience and drive better results.

10. After-Purchase Experience

- **Order Tracking**: Enhance the after-purchase experience by providing users with real-time order tracking updates, allowing them to easily monitor the progress of their orders and ensuring transparency and peace of mind throughout the process.
- **Follow-up Communications**: In addition to order tracking, establish a solid post-purchase relationship with customers by sending personalized thank you emails expressing gratitude for their purchase. Furthermore, it encourages customers to share their feedback and experiences by seeking reviews, which helps improve the quality of products and services and builds trust and credibility. Lastly, leverage customer data and purchase history to offer tailored and relevant product recommendations, creating a personalized shopping experience and increasing the likelihood of future purchases.

Conclusion

An improved user experience is not a one-time objective but an ongoing endeavor. As user expectations change and new technologies arise, e-commerce businesses must stay flexible, constantly striving to simplify, delight, and surpass user expectations. Ultimately, a contented customer is not merely a transaction completed but a potential advocate for the brand.

Walkthrough: Implementing an Enhanced User Experience for an Indian SMB

For an Indian small and medium-sized business (SMB) looking to enhance their user experience (UX) and increase customer satisfaction, here is a step-by-step walkthrough:

1. **Understanding User Needs**: Conduct user research specific to your target audience in India. Consider factors such as demographics, cultural preferences, and shopping behaviors. This will help you tailor your UX enhancements to meet the needs and expectations of Indian customers.

2. **Optimizing Website Load Time**: Ensure your website loads quickly, especially on mobile devices, commonly used for online shopping in India. Optimize images, minimize scripts, and leverage caching techniques to reduce load times.

3. **Designing a Clean and Visually Appealing Website**: Create a clean, uncluttered design that aligns with Indian aesthetic preferences. Consider incorporating vibrant colors, traditional motifs, and culturally relevant imagery to resonate with Indian customers.

4. **Providing High-Quality Images and Detailed Descriptions**: Showcase your products with multiple high-quality images, highlighting their unique features. Create detailed product descriptions in English and local languages, providing comprehensive information to help customers make informed purchasing decisions.

5. **Implementing Responsive Design**: Ensure that your website is fully responsive and mobile-friendly. Given the widespread use of smartphones in India, providing a seamless experience across different devices and screen sizes is essential.

6. **Simplifying Navigation**: Organize your product categories logically and intuitively, considering the preferences and expectations of Indian customers. Implement practical search functionality with auto-suggestions and filters to help users find products quickly.

7. **Building Trust**: Display trust indicators prominently on your website, such as SSL certificates, security badges, and customer reviews. Provide clear and transparent pricing, shipping, and return policies to instill confidence in potential customers.

8. **Enabling Multi-Language and Multi-Currency Support**: Offer language options in regional languages, in addition to English, to cater to a broader audience. Provide currency conversion options to allow customers to view prices and purchase in their preferred currency.

9. **Personalizing the User Experience**: Leverage customer data and browsing history to offer personalized product recommendations. Implement live chat support to provide instant customer assistance and promptly address their queries.

10. **Collecting User Feedback and Analyzing Data**: Regularly collect feedback from Indian customers through surveys, interviews, and user testing sessions. Analyze data from tools like Google Analytics to identify areas for improvement and make data-driven decisions.

11. **Continuous Improvement**: Iterate and enhance your website and user experience based on user feedback, data analysis, and emerging trends in the Indian market. Stay updated with the

latest UX best practices to ensure your SMB remains competitive.

By following this walkthrough and tailoring the strategies mentioned in the chapter to the Indian market, your SMB can enhance the user experience, increase customer satisfaction, and drive sales in India's growing e-commerce landscape.

UX Case Study: Enhancing the User Experience for an Indian SMB

Note: The following case study is a fictional example illustrating how an Indian small and medium-sized business (SMB) implemented the strategies mentioned in the chapter to enhance its user experience (UX) and drive sales.

Client Background

ABC Retail is an Indian SMB specializing in traditional Indian clothing and accessories. With a solid customer base in India and an increasing demand from international customers, ABC Retail recognized the need to improve its online presence and enhance the user experience on its e-commerce website.

Challenge

ABC Retail's website had a high bounce rate, and the conversion rate was lower than expected. They identified the following challenges that needed to be addressed:

1. Slow website load time they are leading to customer frustration and high bounce rates.

2. Lack of personalized product recommendations, resulting in missed cross-selling opportunities.
3. Complex navigation and search functionality make it difficult for customers to find the products they seek.
4. Limited language and currency options, hindering accessibility for non-English speaking and international customers.
5. Insufficient trust indicators reduce customer confidence in online transactions.

Solution

ABC Retail embarked on a project to revamp its website and implement the strategies mentioned in the chapter to enhance the user experience and drive sales. Here is an overview of the solutions they implemented:

1. **Optimizing Website Load Time**: ABC Retail optimized its website's performance by compressing images, minifying CSS and JavaScript files, and leveraging browser caching. As a result, their website load time improved significantly, providing a seamless browsing experience for their customers.
2. **Personalized Product Recommendations**: Leveraging customer browsing history and purchase data, ABC Retail implemented a recommendation engine that displayed personalized product suggestions on the homepage and product pages. This allowed customers to discover relevant products tailored to their preferences, leading to increased engagement and cross-selling opportunities.
3. **Simplified Navigation and Search Functionality**: ABC Retail redesigned its website's navigation menu, categorizing products into clear and intuitive categories and subcategories. They also implemented an advanced search function that

provided auto-suggestions and filters, enabling customers to find products quickly and efficiently.

4. **Expanding Language and Currency Options**: ABC Retail incorporated multiple regional languages and currency options on its website, recognizing the need to cater to a broader audience. Customers could now choose their preferred language and currency, making the shopping experience more accessible and tailored to their needs.

5. **Building Trust with Customers**: ABC Retail prominently displayed trust indicators on its website, including SSL certificates, security badges, and customer reviews. They also implemented a clear and transparent return and refund policy, giving customers confidence and peace of mind when purchasing.

Results

Following implementing these strategies, ABC Retail observed significant improvements in its website's performance and user experience. Key results included:

1. **Reduced Bounce Rates**: The optimized website load time significantly reduced bounce rates, as customers could now browse seamlessly without experiencing delays or frustration.

2. **Increased Conversion Rates**: Personal product recommendations rose in average order value and cross-selling opportunities. Customers were more likely to explore and purchase additional products, improving conversion rates.

3. **Improved Customer Satisfaction**: The simplified navigation and search functionality made it easier for customers to find the products they were looking for, enhancing their overall

satisfaction and reducing the time required for product discovery.

4. **Expanded Customer Base:** By offering multiple language and currency options, ABC Retail attracted a more diverse customer base, including non-English-speaking and international shoppers. This expansion led to increased sales and brand recognition.

5. **Enhanced Trust and Credibility:** Including trust indicators and transparent policies instilled confidence in customers, resulting in higher trust and credibility for ABC Retail. This, in turn, led to increased customer loyalty and positive word-of-mouth referrals.

Conclusion

By prioritizing the user experience and implementing the strategies mentioned in the chapter, ABC Retail successfully enhanced its online presence and improved customer satisfaction. The optimized website load time, personalized product recommendations, simplified navigation, expanded language and currency options, and building customer trust contributed to increased conversion rates, reduced bounce rates, and an expanded customer base.

ABC Retail's commitment to continuous improvement and customer-centric design allowed them to stay ahead in the competitive e-commerce landscape. By constantly monitoring user feedback, analyzing data, and staying updated with emerging UX trends, ABC Retail maintained a user-friendly shopping experience. It solidified their position as a trusted provider of traditional Indian clothing and accessories.

Please note that this case study is a fictional example created for illustrative purposes and does not represent a specific business or client. The strategies and solutions mentioned can be applied to various SMBs in the Indian e-commerce market.

Secure payment gateways and manage logistics

The foundation of every successful e-commerce business lies in its ability to facilitate secure transactions, ensure timely, accurate product deliveries, provide exceptional customer service, and build strong relationships with customers. This chapter will delve into the intricacies of choosing secure payment gateways, exploring different options, and highlighting the importance of selecting a reliable and trustworthy platform. Additionally, it will discuss the challenges that arise in managing e-commerce logistics, such as inventory management, order fulfillment, and shipping, and provide practical solutions to overcome these challenges. By understanding these key areas' complexities and best practices, e-commerce businesses can optimize their operations and enhance the overall customer experience, leading to long-term success and growth.

1. Understanding Payment Gateways

- **What is a Payment Gateway?**: A Payment Gateway is a crucial technology that enables secure online transactions by efficiently transmitting transaction data between websites and banks. It acts as a bridge between customers, merchants, and financial institutions, ensuring smooth and reliable payment processing.

- **Key Features**: When selecting a Payment Gateway for your business, it is essential to consider various key features to enhance your online payment experience. Look for gateways that offer robust fraud prevention mechanisms to protect against unauthorized activities and ensure the safety of both customers and merchants. Additionally, choose a gateway that supports multiple payment options, such as credit cards, debit cards, and digital wallets, to cater to the diverse preferences of your customers. Lastly, seamless integration with your e-commerce platform is crucial for a streamlined and efficient payment process, allowing for a seamless customer experience.

2. Ensuring Transactional Security

To ensure the security of transactions, several measures can be implemented:

- **SSL Certificates**: Secure Socket Layer (SSL) encryption is crucial for transactional security. It guarantees the secure transmission of sensitive data, such as credit card information, between the user's device and the server.
- **Tokenization**: Another effective method to enhance security is tokenization. This process replaces sensitive data with unique tokens like credit cards or bank details. By doing so, the sensitive information is never stored on your servers, reducing the risk of data breaches.
- **Two-Factor Authentication (2FA)**: Implementing two-factor authentication adds a layer of security. With 2FA, users must verify their identity using two different methods, typically a combination of something they know (like a password) and something they have (like a verification code sent to their mobile device). This helps prevent unauthorized access to user accounts and protects against cyber threats.

3. Offering Multiple Payment Options

Expanding on offering multiple payment options, your business must provide various ways for customers to make payments. This enhances customer convenience and increases the likelihood of completing a successful transaction. Here are some essential payment methods that your gateway should support:

- **Credit and Debit Cards**: These are the most commonly used payment methods worldwide. By accepting credit and debit cards, you can cater to a wide range of customers who prefer this convenient and widely accepted payment option.
- **Digital Wallets**: Besides credit and debit cards, offering digital wallets as a payment option is also beneficial. Digital wallets like Apple Pay, Google Wallet, or Samsung Pay provide a seamless and secure way for customers to make payments using their mobile devices. Integrating these popular digital wallets into your payment system can attract tech-savvy customers who prefer quick and easy checkouts.
- **Bank Transfers and EMI**: Bank transfers and Equated Monthly Installments (EMI) are another vital payment option. Bank transfers are beneficial for high-value products or B2B transactions where customers may prefer directly transferring funds from their bank accounts. On the other hand, EMI options allow customers to spread out the purchase cost over time, making it more affordable for them.

By offering these multiple payment options, your business can cater to your customers' diverse needs and preferences, increasing customer satisfaction and higher conversion rates.

4. International Transactions

- **Currency Conversion**: It is crucial to ensure that your gateway can handle multiple currencies if you serve international customers. By offering this feature, you can cater to a broader range of customers from different countries, making it more convenient for them to purchase in their local currency.
- **International Cards**: Another essential aspect is global credit and debit card support. You can significantly expand your market reach by enabling your gateway to accept international cards. This means that customers worldwide can make payments using their preferred payment method, increasing their trust and confidence in your business.

5. Streamlining E-commerce Logistics

- **Inventory Management**: Implementing robust inventory management systems that not only track product stock levels in real-time but also provide insights into demand patterns and forecasting, ensuring that you never run out of stock and can meet customer demands efficiently.
- **Warehouse Solutions**: Investing in advanced warehousing solutions, such as automated picking and packing systems, to streamline order processing and minimize errors. It also optimizes warehouse layout and storage strategies to maximize space utilization and improve operational efficiency.
- **Choosing the Right Shipping Partner**: Carefully select a shipping partner that offers reliable and timely deliveries and provides value-added services such as package tracking, insurance options, and hassle-free returns. Building a solid partnership with your shipping provider can result in cost

savings, improved customer satisfaction, and increased repeat business.

6. Multi-Channel Fulfillment

- **Omni-Channel Experience**: To provide a seamless and convenient shopping experience for your customers, it is essential to have a consistent and efficient fulfillment process across all the platforms you sell on. This includes your website and popular marketplaces like Amazon and eBay. You can enhance customer satisfaction and loyalty by ensuring a unified approach to fulfillment.
- **Centralized Tracking**: It is crucial to have robust systems that track orders and inventory across all your sales channels. This will give you a comprehensive and unified view of your operations, making it easier to manage your inventory, monitor order statuses, and provide accurate and timely information to your customers. By having centralized tracking, you can streamline your operations and improve efficiency.

7. Handling Returns and Refunds

- **Clear and Transparent Return Policy**: Communicating your return and refund policies to your customers is crucial. Ensure your policies are fair, customer-centric, and easy to understand. This will help build trust and confidence in your brand.
- **Streamlined and Hassle-Free Return Process**: To make the return process as seamless as possible for your customers, consider simplifying it further. Besides having a clear return policy, offer additional convenience such as prepaid return labels or free return shipping. By doing so, you not only

enhance customer trust but also make it easier for them to return items if needed.

- **Prompt Refund Processing**: Another critical aspect of handling returns and refunds is to ensure that refunds are processed promptly. Make it a priority to process refunds quickly and efficiently, providing a positive customer experience.

- **Proactive Customer Support**: Besides having clear policies and a streamlined return process, it is essential to provide bold customer support. Be readily available to address any concerns or questions that customers may have regarding returns or refunds. This will further enhance customer satisfaction and loyalty.

- **Continuous Improvement**: Continuously monitor and evaluate your return and refund processes to identify areas for improvement. Gather feedback from customers and use it to enhance your policies and procedures. You can give your customers an exceptional return and refund experience by constantly striving to improve.

Remember, handling returns and refunds is an essential aspect of customer service. By focusing on transparency, convenience, promptness, proactive support, and continuous improvement, you can effectively manage returns and refunds while maintaining a positive customer experience.

8. Scaling Logistics for Growth

- **Expand Warehousing**: As your business experiences rapid growth and an increase in sales volume, it is essential to consider expanding your warehousing solutions. By doing so, you will have the capacity to store more inventory and efficiently fulfill customer orders. This can be achieved by investing in more extensive warehouse facilities or partnering with reliable third-party fulfillment centers. These options will enable you to meet the increasing demand and provide your customers with a seamless order fulfillment experience.

- **Automated Solutions**: Embracing automation in logistics operations can significantly enhance efficiency and productivity, especially during peak sales. Implementing computerized solutions for order processing, labeling, and shipping will dramatically reduce manual errors and save valuable time. By utilizing technology such as barcode scanners, automated sorting systems, and shipping software, you can streamline your logistics processes and ensure the timely delivery of products to your customers. This improves customer satisfaction and allows your business to handle higher order volumes without compromising quality or accuracy.

9. The Role of Technology in Logistics

Technology is crucial in optimizing logistics operations in today's fast-paced and competitive business environment. By leveraging advanced technological solutions, companies can streamline their processes, enhance efficiency, and improve customer satisfaction. Here are a few key ways technology can revolutionize the logistics industry:

- **Integrated Systems:** One of the most significant advancements in logistics technology is integrating various systems. You can seamlessly flow data and information across different channels by integrating your e-commerce platform, payment gateways, and logistics solutions. This integration enables real-time tracking of orders, inventory management, and efficient order fulfillment.

- **AI and Predictive Analysis**: Artificial Intelligence (AI) has proven to be a game-changer in many industries, and logistics is no exception. By harnessing the power of AI and predictive analysis, companies can gain valuable insights into sales trends, customer behavior, and demand patterns. This data can be utilized to optimize inventory management, anticipate shipping demands, and make informed procurement and supply chain management decisions.

Embracing logistics technology improves operational efficiency and enables businesses to stay ahead of the competition. Companies can streamline processes, reduce costs, and provide seamless customer experiences by implementing integrated systems and leveraging AI-driven insights. Technology has become an indispensable tool in the modern logistics landscape, and companies that fail to adapt risk being left behind in the race for success.

10. Continuous Review and Adaptation

Adopting a proactive approach towards the payment and delivery experience is essential to ensure continuous improvement and success. Here are a few key strategies to consider:

- **Feedback Loop**: Establish an effective feedback loop with customers, encouraging them to share their thoughts and suggestions regarding the payment and delivery process. By actively seeking feedback, you can identify areas of improvement and make necessary adjustments to enhance customer satisfaction.

- **Stay Updated:** In today's rapidly evolving logistics and fintech sectors, it is crucial to stay informed about the latest advancements, technologies, and best practices. Regularly monitor industry trends, attend relevant conferences and seminars, and engage with industry experts to stay ahead of the curve. You can identify new opportunities, improve operational efficiency, and optimize your customers' payment and delivery experience by visiting updated.

By implementing these strategies, you can foster a culture of continuous improvement and adaptability, ensuring that your payment and delivery processes are always up-to-date and aligned with industry standards.

Conclusion

A secure and efficient payment and logistics system is crucial for gaining customer trust and encouraging repeat business. By investing in reliable payment gateways and continuously improving logistics, e-commerce businesses can guarantee and provide a shopping experience that meets and surpasses customer expectations.

Practical Example: Benefits for Indian SMBs

For small and medium-sized businesses (SMBs) in India, implementing secure payment gateways and efficient logistics management can positively impact their business operations and growth. Here is a practical example of how these topics can help Indian SMBs:

1. **Enhanced Customer Trust:** By choosing secure payment gateways and implementing robust transactional security measures, Indian SMBs can provide customers with a safe and

trustworthy online shopping experience. This can help build trust and credibility, encouraging customers to purchase and increasing repeat business.

2. **Expanded Customer Base:** Multiple payment options, including popular digital wallets and bank transfers, allow Indian SMBs to cater to customers' diverse needs and preferences. This can attract a broader customer base, including those who prefer alternative payment methods or have limited access to traditional banking systems.

3. **Improved Operational Efficiency:** Implementing effective inventory management systems and optimizing warehouse operations can help Indian SMBs streamline their logistics processes. This leads to better inventory control, reduced stockouts, and improved order fulfillment. As a result, SMBs can efficiently manage their resources, reduce costs, and provide timely product deliveries to customers.

4. **Increased Market Reach:** By accepting international cards and offering currency conversion, Indian SMBs can expand their market reach and attract customers worldwide. This opens up opportunities for cross-border sales and enables SMBs to tap into the global e-commerce market.

5. **Seamless Omni-Channel Experience:** By adopting an omni-channel approach to fulfillment and integrating various platforms, such as websites and popular marketplaces, Indian SMBs can provide a seamless and consistent shopping experience across different channels. This enhances customer satisfaction and loyalty, increasing sales and business growth.

6. **Cost Savings and Efficiency:** Embracing automation and leveraging technology in logistics operations can help Indian SMBs save costs and improve efficiency. Automated order processing, barcode scanning, and shipping software can

minimize errors, reduce manual work, and expedite order fulfillment. This enables SMBs to handle higher order volumes without compromising accuracy or quality.

By implementing the best practices discussed in this chapter, Indian SMBs can optimize their payment and logistics operations, provide exceptional customer experiences, and position themselves for long-term success in the competitive e-commerce landscape.

Walkthrough: Implementing Payment and Logistics Strategies for an Indian SMB

1. **Evaluate Payment Gateway Options**: Research and identify reliable and secure payment gateway providers that cater to Indian businesses. Consider transaction fees, fraud prevention mechanisms, supported payment options, and seamless integration with your e-commerce platform.

2. **Select a Payment Gateway**: Choose a payment gateway that aligns with your business requirements and offers the necessary features discussed in the chapter, such as robust fraud prevention, support for multiple payment options, and seamless integration. Ensure that the gateway supports Indian payment methods like UPI, net banking, and popular digital wallets used in India.

3. **Ensure Transactional Security**: Implement SSL certificates to encrypt sensitive data transmitted between your customers' devices and your server. Explore tokenization options to enhance security by replacing sensitive data with unique tokens. Consider implementing two-factor authentication (2FA) to add an extra layer of protection to customer accounts.

4. **Offer Multiple Payment Options**: Integrate credit and debit card payment processing into your website or platform. Explore partnerships with popular digital wallet providers such as Paytm, PhonePe, and Google Pay. Consider enabling bank transfers and Equated Monthly Installments (EMI) options to cater to a broader range of customers.

5. **Consider International Transactions**: If you plan to serve international customers, ensure your payment gateway supports multi-currency handling. Enable global credit and debit card support to expand your market reach. Provide a seamless experience by offering currency conversion options on your website.

6. **Implement Inventory Management Systems**: Invest in inventory management systems that track stock levels in real time and provide insights into demand patterns. Leverage technology to automate inventory control, reordering, and forecasting processes. This ensures you have the right products in stock and can meet customer demands efficiently.

7. **Optimize Warehouse Operations**: Evaluate your warehouse layout and storage strategies to maximize space utilization and improve operational efficiency. Consider implementing automated picking and packing systems to streamline order processing and minimize errors. Explore partnerships with third-party fulfillment centers for additional storage capacity and efficient order fulfillment.

8. **Choose Reliable Shipping Partners**: Select shipping partners that offer reliable and timely deliveries, package tracking, insurance options, and hassle-free returns. Negotiate competitive shipping rates to minimize costs. Build strong partnerships to benefit from value-added services and enhance customer satisfaction.

9. **Streamline Multi-Channel Fulfillment**: Ensure a consistent and efficient fulfillment process across all your sales channels, including your website and popular marketplaces. Implement centralized tracking systems to monitor orders and inventory across platforms. This provides a unified view of operations and streamlines order management.

10. **Establish Clear Return and Refund Policies**: Communicate your return and refund policies clearly to customers. Ensure they are fair, customer-centric, and easy to understand. Simplify the return process by offering prepaid return labels or free shipping, making it convenient for customers to return items if needed.

11. **Continuously Review and Adapt**: Encourage customers to provide feedback on the payment and delivery experience. Regularly evaluate your processes and policies, seeking areas for improvement. Stay updated with industry trends and best practices to remain competitive and provide an exceptional customer experience.

12. **Embrace Technology**: Leverage integrated systems to streamline data flow between your e-commerce platform, payment gateway, and logistics solutions. Consider utilizing AI-driven insights to optimize inventory management, anticipate shipping demands, and make informed decisions. Explore automation options to enhance efficiency, reduce costs, and improve customer satisfaction.

By following these steps and tailoring them to your specific business needs, an Indian SMB can implement effective payment and logistics strategies. This will help build customer trust, enhance operational efficiency, expand market reach, and drive long-term success in the e-commerce industry.

Case Study: XYZ E-commerce - Enhancing Payment and Logistics for Indian Customers

XYZ E-commerce, an Indian online retailer specializing in fashion and lifestyle products, has successfully implemented the abovementioned strategies to enhance its payment and logistics operations. XYZ E-commerce has achieved significant growth and customer satisfaction by focusing on customer trust, operational efficiency, and market reach.

1. Secure Payment Gateways

XYZ E-commerce partnered with a leading payment gateway provider in India to ensure secure online transactions. They selected a gateway that offered robust fraud prevention mechanisms, seamless integration with their e-commerce platform, and support for multiple payment options, including credit cards, debit cards, net banking, and popular digital wallets like Paytm and PhonePe. This allowed customers to choose their preferred payment method, enhancing convenience and trust.

2. Transactional Security

To ensure the security of customer transactions, XYZ E-commerce implemented SSL certificates to encrypt sensitive data transmitted between customer devices and their servers. They also adopted tokenization, replacing sensitive credit card information with unique tokens. Additionally, they implemented two-factor authentication (2FA) to add an extra layer of security and prevent unauthorized access to customer accounts.

3. Multiple Payment Options

Understanding their customers' diverse needs and preferences, XYZ E-commerce offered multiple payment options. In addition to credit and debit cards, they integrated popular digital wallets like Paytm, PhonePe, and Google Pay. They also enabled net banking for customers who preferred direct bank transfers. By providing these options, XYZ E-commerce catered to a wide range of customers, increasing conversion rates and customer satisfaction.

4. International Transactions

To expand their market reach, XYZ E-commerce implemented support for international transactions. They partnered with payment gateways that offered multi-currency handling, allowing customers worldwide to purchase in their local currency. This feature attracted international customers and increased trust and confidence in the brand.

5. Streamlined Logistics

XYZ E-commerce invested in advanced inventory management systems to efficiently track stock levels, analyze demand patterns, and optimize procurement. They achieved real-time inventory visibility and minimized stockouts by integrating their e-commerce platform with inventory management software. They also collaborated with reliable shipping partners to ensure reliable and timely deliveries. Package tracking, insurance options, and hassle-free returns were provided, enhancing customer satisfaction.

6. Omni-Channel Fulfillment

XYZ E-commerce adopted an omnichannel approach to fulfillment to provide a seamless shopping experience across different channels. They integrated their website with popular marketplaces like Amazon and Flipkart, ensuring consistent order management and fulfillment processes. Centralized tracking systems allowed them to monitor orders and inventory across platforms, providing a unified view of operations.

7. Handling Returns and Refunds

XYZ E-commerce established clear and transparent return and refund policies, communicating them to customers through its website and customer support channels. They simplified the return process by offering prepaid return labels and free return shipping. By promptly processing refunds and providing proactive customer support, they ensured a positive return experience, building trust and loyalty.

8. Scaling Logistics for Growth

As XYZ E-commerce experienced rapid growth, they expanded their warehousing facilities to accommodate increasing inventory. They also embraced automation in their logistics operations, implementing barcode scanners and automated sorting systems. These computerized solutions streamlined order processing, minimized errors, and improved operational efficiency, allowing them to handle higher order volumes without compromising quality.

Conclusion

By implementing secure payment gateways, ensuring transactional security, offering multiple payment options, and streamlining logistics operations, XYZ E-commerce successfully enhanced its payment and delivery experience for Indian customers. Their focus on customer trust, operational efficiency, and market reach has increased sales, customer satisfaction, and long-term growth in the competitive e-commerce industry.

Please note that this case study is fictional and created for illustrative purposes. The name "XYZ E-commerce" is a placeholder and does not represent any authentic brand.

OPERATIONAL EFFICIENCY WITH TECH

Using technology for inventory management

Inventory management is critical to running a small or medium-sized business (SMB) in India. Efficiently managing inventory can help optimize operations, reduce costs, and improve customer satisfaction. One way to achieve effective inventory management is by leveraging technology solutions tailored to Indian SMBs.

1. Implementing an Inventory Management System

An inventory management system is a software tool that enables SMBs to track and control their inventory in real-time. It provides inventory tracking, automated stock updates, and generating reports. Indian SMBs can choose from various inventory management software options available in the market, considering cost, scalability, and ease of use.

2. Barcode and RFID Technology

Using barcode and RFID (Radio-Frequency Identification) technology can streamline inventory management processes for Indian SMBs. Businesses can easily track and manage inventory levels by assigning unique barcodes or RFID tags to each product. This technology enables accurate and efficient inventory counting, minimizing manual errors and saving time.

3. Cloud-Based Inventory Management

Adopting cloud-based inventory management solutions offers several advantages for Indian SMBs. Cloud-based platforms provide real-time access to inventory data from anywhere, facilitating remote inventory monitoring and management. Additionally, cloud-based systems often offer integration capabilities with other business tools, such as accounting software, further streamlining operations.

4. Demand Forecasting and Analytics

Leveraging technology for demand forecasting and analytics can help Indian SMBs optimize their inventory levels. By analyzing historical data, market trends, and customer behavior, businesses can make informed decisions about stock replenishment, reducing the risk of stockouts or overstocking. Advanced analytics tools can also provide insights into inventory turnover, product performance, and profitability.

5. Mobile Inventory Management Apps

With the widespread use of smartphones in India, mobile inventory management apps can be valuable tools for SMBs. These apps allow businesses to manage inventory on the go, enabling tasks such as barcode scanning, order management, and stock updates directly from mobile devices. Mobile apps provide flexibility and convenience, empowering Indian SMBs to efficiently handle inventory management tasks anytime, anywhere.

By embracing technology-driven solutions for inventory management, Indian SMBs can enhance operational efficiency, minimize costs, and improve overall business performance. It is essential for SMBs to carefully evaluate their specific requirements and select the most suitable technology solutions to meet their inventory management needs.

Here is a walkthrough on how an Indian company can achieve effective inventory management using technology solutions:

1. **Assess Your Needs:** Evaluate your inventory management requirements and identify the challenges you must address. Consider factors such as the size of your business, the types of products you sell, and your projected growth.

2. **Choose an Inventory Management System:** Select an inventory management system that meets your business needs. Look for features like real-time inventory tracking, automated stock updates, and reporting capabilities. Consider software options tailored for Indian SMBs, considering cost, scalability, and ease of use.

3. **Implement Barcode and RFID Technology:** Integrate barcode and RFID technology into your inventory management processes. Assign unique barcodes or RFID tags to each product for efficient tracking and management. This technology helps streamline inventory counting, minimize errors, and save time.

4. **Explore Cloud-Based Solutions:** Consider adopting cloud-based inventory management solutions. These platforms provide real-time access to inventory data, allowing for remote monitoring and management. Look for systems that offer integration capabilities with other business tools, such as accounting software, to streamline operations further.

5. **Utilize Demand Forecasting and Analytics:** Leverage technology for demand forecasting and analytics. Analyze

historical data, market trends, and customer behavior to make informed decisions about stock replenishment. Advanced analytics tools can provide insights into inventory turnover, product performance, and profitability.

6. **Utilize Mobile Inventory Management Apps:** Take advantage of mobile inventory management apps. These apps allow you to manage inventory on the go, with features like barcode scanning, order management, and stock updates directly from mobile devices. This flexibility and convenience enable efficient inventory management tasks anytime, anywhere.

7. **Train and Educate Employees:** Provide proper training and education to your employees on effectively using the technology solutions implemented. Ensure they understand the system's functionalities and how to utilize them to optimize inventory management processes.

8. **Monitor and Evaluate:** Continuously monitor and evaluate the effectiveness of your inventory management system. Regularly review reports and analyze key performance indicators to identify areas for improvement. Make necessary adjustments and optimizations to enhance operational efficiency.

By following these steps, Indian SMBs can successfully leverage inventory management technology, optimize operations, reduce costs, and improve overall business performance.

Case Study: XYZ Retail - Transforming Inventory Management with Technology

Introduction

XYZ Retail, a leading Indian SMB in the retail industry, faced significant challenges in managing its inventory efficiently. They needed help with stockouts, overstocking, and manual errors, increasing costs and customer dissatisfaction. To address these issues, XYZ Retail embarked on a journey to leverage technology-driven solutions for inventory management.

Implementation of an Inventory Management System

XYZ Retail implemented an advanced inventory management system tailored for Indian SMBs. The design provided real-time inventory tracking, automated stock updates, and comprehensive reporting capabilities. This gave XYZ Retail a holistic view of its inventory, enabling better decision-making and reducing the risk of stockouts or overstocking.

Integration of Barcode and RFID Technology

XYZ Retail integrated barcode and RFID technology to streamline inventory management processes. Every product was assigned a unique barcode or RFID tag, enabling accurate tracking and efficient management. This technology eliminated manual errors, improved inventory counting accuracy, and saved significant time in stocktaking procedures.

Adoption of Cloud-Based Inventory Management

XYZ Retail embraced cloud-based inventory management solutions to enhance its operations. The cloud-based platform provided real-time access to inventory data from anywhere, allowing XYZ Retail to monitor and manage its inventory remotely. Integration capabilities with other business tools, such as accounting software, further streamlined operations and improved overall efficiency.

Utilization of Demand Forecasting and Analytics

Leveraging technology for demand forecasting and analytics, XYZ Retail gained valuable insights into its inventory needs. They could accurately forecast demand and make informed decisions about stock replenishment by analyzing historical data, market trends, and customer behavior. This reduced the risk of stockouts and optimized inventory levels, leading to improved customer satisfaction and increased profitability.

Implementation of Mobile Inventory Management Apps

Recognizing the ubiquity of smartphones in India, XYZ Retail implemented mobile inventory management apps. These apps empowered their employees to manage inventory on the go using features like barcode scanning, order management, and stock updates directly from their mobile devices. This flexibility and convenience enabled XYZ Retail to handle inventory management tasks efficiently, even outside the physical store premises.

Results and Benefits

The implementation of technology-driven solutions revolutionized XYZ Retail's inventory management practices and yielded significant benefits:

1. Improved Operational Efficiency: Real-time inventory tracking, automated stock updates, and streamlined processes resulted in enhanced operational efficiency. XYZ Retail could effectively manage its inventory, reducing stockouts and optimizing stock levels.

2. Cost Reduction: By minimizing manual errors, eliminating stockouts, and preventing overstocking, XYZ Retail significantly reduced costs associated with inventory management. They could allocate resources more efficiently, resulting in cost savings.

3. Enhanced Customer Satisfaction: Accurate inventory tracking and efficient order fulfillment improved customer satisfaction. XYZ Retail could meet customer demands promptly, ensuring product availability and a seamless shopping experience.

4. Data-Driven Decision Making: With access to comprehensive reports and analytics, XYZ Retail gained valuable insights into its inventory performance. They could make data-driven decisions, optimize stock levels, and identify growth opportunities.

Conclusion

By strategically implementing technology solutions, XYZ Retail successfully transformed its inventory management practices. By leveraging an inventory management system, barcode and RFID technology, cloud-based solutions, demand forecasting, and mobile apps, they achieved efficient operations, reduced costs, and improved customer satisfaction. XYZ Retail is a remarkable case study for other Indian SMBs looking to optimize their inventory management processes through technology-driven solutions.

Streamlining HR processes using software

In recent years, the use of software has become increasingly popular in streamlining HR processes for small and medium-sized businesses (SMBs) in India. By leveraging technology, Indian SMBs can optimize their HR operations, improve efficiency, and enhance employee experiences. Here are some key areas where software can be utilized to streamline HR processes:

1. Recruitment and Onboarding

Software solutions can automate and simplify the recruitment and onboarding processes for Indian SMBs. From creating job postings and managing applications to conducting online interviews and facilitating document verification, HR software can significantly reduce the time and effort involved in hiring new employees. Additionally, it can provide a seamless onboarding experience by automating the creation of employee profiles, managing paperwork, and delivering necessary training materials.

2. Employee Data Management

Maintaining accurate and up-to-date employee data is crucial for HR departments. HR software can centralize employee information, including personal details, job history, performance records, and leave balances. This eliminates the need for manual record-keeping and enables easy access to employee data, simplifying administrative tasks such as generating reports, tracking attendance, and managing leave requests.

3. Payroll and Benefits Administration

Managing payroll and employee benefits can be complex and time-consuming for Indian SMBs. HR software can automate payroll calculations, tax deductions, and salary disbursements, ensuring accuracy and compliance with legal requirements. Additionally, it can streamline benefits administration by allowing employees to make benefit selections, tracking usage, and facilitating seamless communication between HR and benefits providers.

4. Performance Management

Performance management is essential for evaluating employee performance, setting goals, and providing feedback. HR software can facilitate the entire performance management cycle, from goal setting and performance reviews to performance tracking and development planning. It can automate performance appraisal processes, provide real-time performance insights, and enable continuous feedback, fostering a culture of growth and development within the organization.

5. Employee Self-Service

Empowering employees with self-service capabilities can significantly streamline HR processes. HR software can provide a user-friendly interface for employees to access and update their personal information, request leaves, view payslips, and access company policies.

By enabling self-service, Indian SMBs can reduce the administrative burden on HR teams and enhance employee satisfaction and engagement.

Implementing HR software tailored to the specific needs of Indian SMBs can bring numerous benefits. However, it is essential to evaluate software options carefully, considering factors such as affordability, scalability, data security, and user-friendliness. By embracing technology and leveraging HR software, Indian SMBs can streamline their HR processes, save time and resources, and focus on strategic initiatives to drive organizational growth.

Here is a walkthrough of how an Indian SMB can streamline their HR processes using software:

1. **Identify HR Pain Points**: Identify your HR department's specific pain points and challenges. This could include recruitment, onboarding, employee data management, payroll, benefits administration, and performance management.

2. **Research HR Software Solutions**: Conduct thorough research to identify HR software solutions that cater to the needs of Indian SMBs. Look for features such as recruitment management, employee data management, payroll processing, benefits administration, and performance management tools. Consider factors like affordability, scalability, data security, and user-friendliness when evaluating different software options.

3. **Select and Implement the Software**: Once you have identified the HR software that aligns with your requirements, proceed with selecting and implementing it. Collaborate with your IT team or software vendor to ensure a smooth implementation. Customize the software to suit your HR processes and integrate it with existing systems.

4. **Recruitment and Onboarding**: Utilize the software to automate and streamline your recruitment and onboarding processes. Create job postings, manage applications, conduct online interviews, verify documents, and generate employment contracts or offer letters—Automate onboarding by creating employee profiles, handling paperwork, and providing necessary training materials.

5. **Employee Data Management**: Centralize employee data using the software. Store personal details, job history, performance records, and leave balances in one secure location. Enable employees to access and update their information, reducing the administrative burden on HR. Generate reports, track attendance, and manage leave requests effortlessly.

6. **Payroll and Benefits Administration**: Leverage the software to simplify payroll and benefits administration. Automate payroll calculations, tax deductions, and salary disbursements, ensuring accuracy and compliance. Allow employees to make benefit selections, track usage, and communicate with benefits providers seamlessly.

7. **Performance Management**: Streamline performance management using the software. Set goals, conduct performance reviews, track progress, and provide feedback within the system. Automate performance appraisal processes, gain real-time insights, and encourage continuous feedback and development planning.

8. **Employee Self-Service**: Enable employees to access self-service capabilities through the software. Provide a user-friendly interface for employees to manage their personal information, request leaves, view payslips, and access company policies. Empowering employees with self-service options reduces the

administrative burden on HR and enhances employee satisfaction and engagement.

9. **Training and Support**: Ensure that your HR team and employees receive adequate training on using the software effectively. Provide ongoing support and resources to address any queries or issues that may arise during the implementation and usage of the software.

Following this walkthrough, Indian SMBs can effectively streamline their HR processes using software, save time and resources, and focus on strategic initiatives to drive organizational growth.

Case Study: XYZ Company - Streamlining HR Processes with Software

Overview

XYZ Company, a growing Indian SMB, faced challenges in managing its HR processes efficiently. They needed help with manual record-keeping, time-consuming administrative tasks, and a need for centralized employee data. XYZ Company implemented HR software tailored to their needs to address these pain points.

Objectives

1. Streamline recruitment and onboarding processes.
2. Centralize employee data management.
3. Simplify payroll and benefits administration.
4. Enhance performance management.
5. Empower employees with self-service capabilities.

Solution

After careful evaluation, XYZ Company selected an HR software solution that offered comprehensive features for their requirements. They customized the software to align with their HR processes and integrated it with their existing systems.

Recruitment and Onboarding

With the HR software, XYZ Company automated its recruitment and onboarding processes. They created job postings, managed applications, conducted online interviews, and verified documents within the system. Additionally, the software facilitated the seamless creation of employee profiles, ordering paperwork, and delivering training materials during onboarding.

Employee Data Management

The HR software enabled XYZ Company to centralize employee data, including personal details, job history, performance records, and leave balances. This eliminated the need for manual record-keeping and provided easy access to employee information. Generating reports, tracking attendance, and managing leave requests became effortless tasks.

Payroll and Benefits Administration

Automating payroll calculations, tax deductions, and salary disbursements became hassle-free with the HR software. XYZ Company ensured accuracy and compliance while simplifying payroll management. The software also streamlined benefits administration by allowing employees to make benefit selections, tracking usage, and facilitating communication between HR and benefits providers.

Performance Management

The performance management process at XYZ Company was transformed with the HR software. They set goals, conducted performance reviews, and tracked employee progress within the system. The software's automated performance appraisal processes provided real-time insights and encouraged continuous feedback and development planning.

Employee Self-Service

Empowering employees with self-service capabilities improved HR processes at XYZ Company. Employees could access and update their personal information, request leaves, view payslips, and access company policies through the software. This reduced the administrative burden on HR, increased employee satisfaction, and improved engagement.

Results

Implementing HR software tailored to their needs brought significant improvements to significantly improved XYZ Company's HR processes. They experienced:

- Reduced administrative burden: Manual tasks were automated, saving time and resources.
- Improved data accuracy: Centralized employee data eliminated the risk of errors.

- Enhanced efficiency: Streamlined processes increased productivity and reduced delays.
- Better employee experiences: Self-service capabilities and streamlined onboarding improved employee satisfaction.
- Strategic focus: With HR processes streamlined, XYZ Company could focus on strategic initiatives for organizational growth.

By leveraging HR software, XYZ Company successfully streamlined its HR processes, improved efficiency, and enhanced employee experiences. They continue to evolve their HR practices, leveraging technology to drive their business forward.

Efficient finance management through digital tools

Efficient Finance Management for Indian SMBs Using Digital Tools

In today's digital age, small and medium-sized businesses (SMBs) in India have access to a wide range of digital tools that can help streamline and enhance their finance management processes. By leveraging these tools effectively, Indian SMBs can achieve greater efficiency, accuracy, and control over their financial operations.

1. Automated Bookkeeping and Accounting

Digital tools, including accounting software and cloud-based platforms, have revolutionized bookkeeping for Indian SMBs. These tools allow businesses to monitor their income, expenses, and financial transactions in real time. Additionally, these innovative solutions offer a range of features, such as automated financial reporting, efficient invoice management, and simplified tax compliance processes. As a result, Indian SMBs can save significant amounts of time and effort while ensuring accurate financial records and streamlined operations.

2. Online Payment and Invoicing Solutions

Indian small and medium-sized businesses (SMBs) can gain numerous advantages by adopting digital payment and invoicing solutions. By embracing online payment methods, companies can enhance their cash flow and significantly reduce the time it takes to process payments. Moreover, this enables them to offer greater convenience to their customers, as they can now easily make payments from the comfort of their homes or offices. Additionally, online invoicing tools bring further benefits by automating the entire invoicing process. These tools allow businesses to effortlessly generate and send invoices, keep track of payments, and even send automated reminders to their clients. By streamlining and automating these tasks, companies ensure that payments are made promptly while minimizing manual errors.

3. Expense Tracking and Budgeting

Digital expense tracking tools have become increasingly popular among Indian small and medium-sized businesses (SMBs). These tools provide a convenient and efficient way for SMBs to monitor and categorize expenses. By allowing companies to capture receipts digitally and automatically organize costs, these tools enable SMBs to gain valuable insights into their spending patterns.

One of the key benefits of using digital expense tracking tools is the ability to make data-driven decisions. With the help of these tools, SMBs can analyze their expenses more organized and systematically. This allows them to identify areas where they can optimize costs and make informed financial decisions.

Moreover, these tools also offer integrated budgeting features specifically designed to assist SMBs in managing their finances. SMBs can set financial goals, track their budget adherence, and receive alerts when they are nearing their spending limits. This helps SMBs stay on track with their financial plans and make necessary adjustments when needed.

In summary, digital expense tracking tools have revolutionized how Indian SMBs manage their expenses. These tools provide a range of benefits, from efficient expense monitoring and categorization to data-driven decision-making and budget management. By leveraging these tools, SMBs can streamline their financial processes and drive better economic outcomes.

4. Financial Analytics and Reporting

Digital tools with advanced financial analytics and reporting capabilities have revolutionized how Indian small and medium-sized businesses (SMBs) manage their financial health. These tools offer a wide range of features and functionalities that enable companies to gain a comprehensive and in-depth understanding of their financial performance.

With these tools, Indian SMBs can generate highly customizable reports and visualizations that provide detailed insights into their financial metrics. This allows businesses to analyze key performance indicators, track economic trends, and identify areas of improvement. By leveraging these insights, companies can make well-informed, data-driven decisions that drive growth and success.

Furthermore, these digital tools are crucial in strategic planning and forecasting. By utilizing the power of financial analytics, businesses can accurately forecast future economic scenarios, identify potential risks, and develop contingency plans. This proactive approach enables enterprises to stay ahead of the competition and confidently navigate uncertainties.

In addition to managing day-to-day operations, these tools help Indian SMBs identify growth opportunities. Businesses can identify untapped markets, new customer segments, and innovative product/service offerings by analyzing financial data and market trends. This enables enterprises to expand their reach, diversify their revenue streams, and capitalize on emerging opportunities.

In summary, the availability of digital tools with advanced financial analytics and reporting capabilities has revolutionized how Indian SMBs manage their financial health. These tools empower businesses with valuable insights, strategic planning capabilities, and the ability to identify growth opportunities. By leveraging these tools effectively, Indian SMBs can drive sustainable growth, enhance their competitiveness, and achieve long-term success.

5. Secure Data Management and Compliance

Data security and compliance are paramount for Indian small and medium-sized businesses (SMBs). In today's digital age, where cyber threats are rising, SMBS must safeguard their sensitive financial information. Digital finance management tools provide a reliable solution by offering secure data storage and encryption measures. This ensures that valuable financial data is protected from unauthorized access or breaches.

Furthermore, these tools go beyond just data security. They also assist businesses in meeting their tax compliance obligations. By integrating tax compliance features, these tools help SMBs stay updated with the ever-changing regulatory requirements. This saves time and effort and minimizes the risk of non-compliance penalties.

In addition to data security and tax compliance, digital finance management tools also help streamline the tax filing processes for SMBs. With automated features and user-friendly interfaces, these tools simplify the complex tax preparation and submission task. This allows SMBs to focus on their core operations and eliminate the hassle of manual calculations and paperwork.

In conclusion, digital finance management tools are crucial in ensuring the data security and compliance of Indian SMBs. By offering secure data storage, encryption, tax compliance features, and streamlined tax filing processes, these tools provide a comprehensive solution for SMBs to manage their finances effectively and efficiently.

By embracing these digital tools and incorporating them into their finance management practices, Indian SMBs can streamline operations, improve accuracy, and make informed financial decisions, ultimately driving their growth and success in today's competitive business landscape.

Implementation

To implement efficient finance management using digital tools, Indian SMBs can follow these steps:

1. **Assess Business Needs**: Evaluate your finance management requirements and identify areas where digital tools can streamline processes and improve efficiency. Consider bookkeeping, payment and invoicing, expense tracking, budgeting, financial analytics, reporting, and data security.

2. **Research and Select Tools**: Conduct a thorough investigation to identify digital tools that align with your business needs. Look for accounting software, cloud-based platforms, online payment and invoicing solutions, expense-tracking tools, and financial analytics platforms. Consider features, ease of use, scalability, integration capabilities, and customer reviews.

3. **Implement Accounting Software**: Choose an accounting software that suits your business size and requirements. Set up your chart of accounts, input financial data, and automate processes such as income and expense tracking, financial reporting, and tax compliance.

4. **Adopt Online Payment and Invoicing Solutions**: Select a secure online payment gateway and invoicing tool to streamline payment processes. Integrate these tools with your accounting software for seamless tracking and reconciliation of payments.

5. **Utilize Expense Tracking Tools**: Implement digital expense tracking tools to capture and categorize expenses. Explore tools that offer features such as receipt scanning, expense categorization, and budget tracking. Integrate these tools with your accounting software for accurate financial insights.

6. **Leverage Financial Analytics and Reporting**: Implement a financial analytics platform to gain insights into your business's economic performance. Customize reports and visualizations to track key performance indicators, identify trends, and make data-driven decisions.

7. **Ensure Data Security and Compliance**: Choose digital tools prioritizing data security and compliance. Look for secure data storage, encryption, and tax compliance functionalities. Regularly update your devices to stay compliant with changing regulations.

8. **Train and Educate Employees**: Train employees on effectively using the selected digital tools. Ensure they understand the importance of accurate data entry, security protocols, and compliance requirements.

9. **Monitor and Evaluate**: Continuously monitor the effectiveness of the implemented digital tools. Regularly review financial reports, analyze key metrics, and assess the impact on efficiency and accuracy. Make adjustments as needed to optimize processes.

By following these steps, Indian SMBs can implement efficient finance management using digital tools. This will enable them to streamline operations, improve accuracy, make informed financial decisions, and drive growth in today's competitive business landscape.

Case Study: XYZ Retail - Streamlining Finance Management with Digital Tools

Overview

XYZ Retail is a medium-sized retail business based in India. With multiple stores nationwide, XYZ Retail faced challenges in efficiently managing its finance operations, which impacted its overall business performance. To address these challenges, they decided to implement digital tools for finance management.

Challenges

Before adopting digital tools, XYZ Retail encountered several pain points:

1. Manual Bookkeeping: The company relied on manual bookkeeping processes, which were time-consuming and prone to errors. This resulted in delays in financial reporting and difficulty accurately tracking income and expenses.
2. Inefficient Payment Processing: Processing payments from customers took a long time due to manual payment methods, leading to delays in cash flow and customer dissatisfaction.
3. Complex Expense Tracking: Tracking and categorizing expenses across multiple stores was challenging. This made it difficult for XYZ Retail to analyze spending patterns and identify cost-saving opportunities.

Solution

XYZ Retail implemented the following digital tools to streamline their finance management processes:

1. **Accounting Software**: They adopted a cloud-based accounting software that automated their bookkeeping processes. This software allowed them to track income, expenses, and financial transactions in real-time, eliminating the need for manual data entry.
2. **Online Payment Gateway**: XYZ Retail integrated an online payment gateway into its website and point-of-sale systems. This enabled customers to make payments conveniently and securely, reducing the time to process payments and improving cash flow.
3. **Expense Tracking Tool**: They implemented a digital expense tracking tool to capture receipts digitally and automatically categorize expenses. This streamlined their expense tracking process and provided valuable insights into their spending patterns.

Results

By leveraging digital tools for finance management, XYZ Retail achieved the following outcomes:

1. **Improved Efficiency**: The automation of bookkeeping processes saved time and reduced errors. XYZ Retail could generate financial reports more quickly and make informed business decisions based on accurate data.
2. **Enhanced Cash Flow**: Adopting an online payment gateway significantly reduced the time taken to process payments—this improved cash flow and enhanced customer satisfaction by providing a seamless payment experience.
3. **Better Expense Management**: The expense tracking tool enabled XYZ Retail to track and categorize expenses effortlessly. They gained valuable insights into their spending patterns, identified cost-saving opportunities, and made informed decisions to optimize their budget.

Conclusion

By embracing digital tools for finance management, XYZ Retail successfully streamlined its operations and improved its overall financial performance. Automating bookkeeping, efficient payment processing, and effective expense tracking allowed them to save time, enhance cash flow, and optimize expenses.

This case study demonstrates the significant benefits that Indian SMBs can achieve by adopting digital tools for finance management. Following XYZ Retail's example, businesses can overcome challenges, improve efficiency, and make informed financial decisions to drive growth and success in today's competitive business landscape.

HARNESSING DATA FOR BUSINESS GROWTH

Introduction to analytics and data interpretation

This chapter will explore the fundamentals of analytics and data interpretation specifically tailored for small and medium-sized businesses (SMBs). Analytics is crucial in today's business landscape, providing valuable insights and driving informed decision-making. By understanding the basics of analytics and data interpretation, SMBs can unlock the potential of their data to gain a competitive advantage.

1. Understanding Analytics

What is Analytics?

Analytics collects, organizes, analyzes, and interprets data to gain insights and make data-driven decisions. It involves various techniques, tools, and methodologies to uncover patterns, trends, and correlations in data.

Why is Analytics Important for SMBs?

Analytics empowers SMBs to make informed decisions based on data rather than relying solely on intuition or guesswork. By leveraging analytics, SMBs can identify growth opportunities, optimize operations, improve customer experiences, and enhance overall business performance.

2. Key Concepts in Data Interpretation

Data Sources and Collection

Data can be collected from various sources, including customer interactions, sales transactions, website analytics, social media, etc. Identifying relevant data sources and establishing efficient data collection processes is essential to ensure data accuracy and completeness.

Data Analysis Techniques

Data analysis techniques allow SMBs to extract meaningful insights from raw data. These techniques include descriptive analysis to summarize and describe data, diagnostic analysis to understand the causes of specific outcomes, predictive analysis to forecast future trends, and prescriptive analysis to provide recommendations for optimal decision-making.

Data Visualization

Data visualization is the graphical representation of data, making complex information more accessible and understandable. It helps SMBs communicate insights effectively and enables stakeholders to grasp patterns and trends quickly.

3. Implementing Analytics in SMBs

Setting Goals and Defining Metrics

Before diving into analytics, SMBs should define clear goals and identify relevant metrics to measure success. This ensures that analytics efforts align with business objectives and provide actionable insights.

Choosing the Right Tools and Technologies

Selecting appropriate analytics tools and technologies is crucial for SMBs. Consider budget, scalability, ease of use, and compatibility with existing systems when choosing analytics solutions.

Building a Data-Driven Culture

SMBs should foster a data-driven culture within their organization to fully leverage analytics. This involves promoting data literacy, encouraging data-driven decision-making at all levels, and investing in training and resources to build analytical capabilities.

Conclusion

This chapter provided an overview of analytics and data interpretation tailored to SMBs. By embracing analytics and effectively interpreting data, SMBs can gain valuable insights, make informed decisions, and thrive in today's data-driven business environment.

Implementation

To implement analytics and data interpretation in SMBs, follow these steps:

1. **Step 1: Define Business Goals**: Start by clearly defining your business goals. Identify the key areas where analytics can provide insights and support decision-making.
2. **Step 2: Identify Relevant Data Sources**: Determine the relevant data sources for your business goals. This may include customer interactions, sales data, website analytics, and social media data.
3. **Step 3: Establish Data Collection Processes**: Establish efficient data collection processes to ensure accurate and comprehensive data. Use tools and technologies to automate data collection where possible.
4. **Step 4: Choose Analytics Tools**: Select appropriate tools based on your budget, scalability needs, ease of use, and compatibility with existing systems. Consider tools that offer data visualization, predictive analysis, and reporting capabilities.
5. **Step 5: Analyze and Interpret Data**: Apply data analysis techniques to extract insights from your collected data. Use descriptive analysis to summarize and describe data, diagnostic study to understand causes, predictive analysis to forecast trends, and prescriptive analysis to provide recommendations.
6. **Step 6: Visualize Data**: Utilize data visualization techniques to present insights in a visually appealing and easily understandable manner. This helps stakeholders quickly grasp patterns and trends.
7. **Step 7: Set Key Performance Indicators (KPIs)**: Define relevant metrics and KPIs that align with your business goals. These metrics will help you measure the success and impact of your analytics efforts.
8. **Step 8: Monitor and Iterate**: Continuously monitor and analyze your data, making necessary adjustments and

improvements. Regularly review your KPIs and make data-driven decisions to drive business growth.

9. **Step 9: Foster a Data-Driven Culture**: Encourage a data-driven culture within your organization. Promote data literacy and provide training and resources to build analytical capabilities among your team members.

By following these steps, SMBs can effectively implement analytics and data interpretation, gaining valuable insights and making informed decisions to thrive in today's data-driven business environment.

Case Study: Improving Customer Satisfaction through Data-Driven Insights

Background

A small e-commerce business, XYZ Clothing, faced challenges in understanding customers' preferences and improving their shopping experience. They wanted to identify areas of improvement and make data-driven decisions to enhance customer satisfaction.

Step 1: Define Business Goals

XYZ Clothing defined its business goal as improving customer satisfaction by optimizing the online shopping experience and product offerings.

Step 2: Identify Relevant Data Sources

They identified key data sources, including customer feedback surveys, website analytics, and sales data, to gain insights into customer behavior and preferences.

Step 3: Establish Data Collection Processes

XYZ Clothing implemented automated data collection processes by integrating customer feedback surveys and website analytics tools. This ensured accurate and comprehensive data collection.

Step 4: Choose Analytics Tools

They selected an analytics tool that provided features for data visualization, customer segmentation, and trend analysis. This tool allowed them to analyze and interpret their collected data effectively.

Step 5: Analyze and Interpret Data

Using the selected analytics tool, XYZ Clothing performed descriptive and diagnostic analysis on their customer feedback and website analytics data. They gained insights into customer preferences, pain points, and browsing behavior.

Step 6: Visualize Data

They utilized data visualization techniques to create interactive dashboards and reports. This helped them present insights to stakeholders in an easily understandable manner.

Step 7: Set Key Performance Indicators (KPIs)

XYZ Clothing defined KPIs such as customer satisfaction scores, conversion rates, and average order value to measure the success of their initiatives.

Step 8: Monitor and Iterate

They continuously monitored customer feedback, website analytics, and sales data to track the impact of their improvements. They made data-driven decisions to iterate and optimize their online shopping experience.

Step 9: Foster a Data-Driven Culture

XYZ Clothing promoted a data-driven culture within their organization. They trained their team members on data analysis and interpretation, encouraging data-driven decision-making at all levels.

Results

By implementing analytics and data interpretation, XYZ Clothing significantly improved customer satisfaction. They were able to:

- Identify popular product categories and optimize their inventory management.
- Personalize product recommendations based on customer preferences, leading to increased sales.
- Improve website navigation and user experience, resulting in higher conversion rates.
- Address customer pain points and resolve issues promptly, enhancing overall customer satisfaction.

Through their data-driven approach, XYZ Clothing gained a competitive advantage in the e-commerce market and witnessed customer loyalty and revenue growth.

Conclusion

This case study showcases how XYZ Clothing, a small e-commerce business, successfully leveraged analytics and data interpretation to improve customer satisfaction. Collecting and analyzing relevant data gave them valuable insights into customer preferences and behavior, allowing them to make informed decisions and enhance their business performance.

Customer relationship management (CRM) tools

Customer relationship management (CRM) tools are crucial in managing and optimizing customer interactions for small and medium-sized businesses (SMBs). These tools provide a systematic approach to organizing and analyzing customer data, streamlining sales processes, and enhancing customer satisfaction.

Benefits of CRM Tools for SMBs

Implementing CRM tools can bring several benefits to SMBs, including:

1. Improved Customer Insights: CRM tools enable SMBs to gather and analyze customer data, providing valuable insights into customer behavior, preferences, and needs. This information helps businesses tailor their products, services, and marketing strategies to meet customer expectations better.

2. Streamlined Sales Processes: CRM tools automate and streamline sales processes, allowing SMBs to manage leads, track opportunities, and close deals efficiently. By centralizing customer information and interactions, CRM tools enhance collaboration among sales teams and improve overall sales efficiency.

3. Enhanced Customer Service: CRM tools enable SMBs to provide personalized and responsive customer service. By

storing customer interactions, preferences, and purchase history in one place, businesses can deliver timely and tailored support, improving customer satisfaction and loyalty.

4. Increased Efficiency and Productivity: CRM tools automate manual tasks, such as data entry, follow-ups, and reporting, freeing up time for SMBs to focus on core business activities. This increased efficiency and productivity can lead to improved business performance and growth.

Key Features of CRM Tools for SMBs

When choosing CRM tools for SMBs, it is essential to consider the following key features:

1. Contact and Lead Management: The CRM tool should provide a centralized database for storing and managing customer contacts, leads, and prospects. It should enable easy segmentation and categorizing of contacts for targeted marketing and sales efforts.

2. Sales and Opportunity Tracking: The CRM tool should offer features for tracking sales opportunities, pipeline management, and forecasting. It should provide insights into the sales process, helping SMBs identify bottlenecks and optimize sales strategies.

3. Customer Service and Support: The CRM tool should facilitate efficient customer service and support by enabling ticket management, case tracking, and knowledge base management. It should empower SMBs to deliver timely and practical support to their customers.

4. Reporting and Analytics: The CRM tool should provide robust reporting and analytics capabilities, allowing SMBs to track key

performance metrics, measure sales effectiveness, and gain actionable insights into customer behavior and trends.

5. Integration and Customization: The CRM tool should integrate seamlessly with other essential business tools, such as email marketing platforms, e-commerce systems, and accounting software. It should also offer customization options to adapt to the specific needs and workflows of SMBs.

Choosing the Right CRM Tool for Your SMB

Selecting the right CRM tool for your SMB requires careful evaluation of your business requirements, budget, and scalability needs. Consider factors such as ease of use, scalability, customer support, and pricing models before deciding. It is also beneficial to try out free trials or demos to assess the usability and suitability of the CRM tool for your SMB.

Implementing a suitable CRM tool allows SMBs to streamline their customer relationship management processes, improve customer satisfaction, and drive business growth.

Case Study: XYZ Company's Success with CRM Tools

Introduction

In this case study, we will explore how XYZ Company, a small manufacturing business, successfully implemented CRM tools to enhance customer relationship management processes and drive business growth.

Challenge

Before implementing CRM tools, XYZ Company faced challenges managing customer interactions and tracking sales opportunities. Their existing manual processes led to inefficiencies, limited customer insights, and missed business opportunities.

Solution

XYZ Company decided to adopt a CRM tool specifically designed for SMBs. They chose a cloud-based CRM solution offering comprehensive contact management, sales tracking, and customer service features.

Implementation

XYZ Company initiated the implementation process by importing customer data into the CRM tool. They organized contacts, leads, and opportunities, ensuring accurate and up-to-date information. The CRM tool allowed them to segment their customer base effectively, enabling targeted marketing and sales efforts.

Results

By implementing CRM tools, XYZ Company achieved significant improvements in their customer relationship management processes:

1. Enhanced Customer Insights: The CRM tool provided XYZ Company with valuable customer insights, enabling them to understand customer preferences, purchase history, and behavior. This information allowed them to tailor their product offerings and marketing strategies, increasing customer satisfaction and loyalty.

2. Streamlined Sales Processes: The CRM tool automated the sales pipeline, allowing XYZ Company to manage leads, track opportunities, and forecast sales efficiently. The centralized platform improved collaboration among sales teams, increased efficiency, and enabled effective sales strategies.

3. Improved Customer Service: With the CRM tool's customer service features, XYZ Company was able to provide personalized and timely support. Customer interactions, inquiries, and cases were seamlessly tracked and managed, enhancing customer satisfaction and retention.

4. Increased Efficiency and Productivity: The automation provided by the CRM tool significantly reduced manual tasks, such as data entry and reporting. This allowed XYZ Company's employees to focus on core business activities, increasing productivity and overall business growth.

Conclusion

By successfully implementing CRM tools, XYZ Company transformed its customer relationship management processes and achieved remarkable results. By gathering customer insights, streamlining sales processes, and improving customer service, they experienced increased customer satisfaction, sales performance, and overall business growth.

If your SMB is facing similar challenges, considering the adoption of CRM tools could be a game-changer for your business success.

Pros of CRM Tools for SMBs	Cons of CRM Tools for SMBs
Improved customer insights	Initial setup and learning curve
Streamlined sales processes	Cost of implementation and subscription

Pros of CRM Tools for SMBs	Cons of CRM Tools for SMBs
Enhanced customer service	Integration challenges with existing systems
Increased efficiency and productivity	Potential resistance from employees
Robust reporting and analytics capabilities	Data security and privacy concerns

To address the cons of CRM tools for SMBs, consider the following strategies:

1. **Initial setup and learning curve**: Provide comprehensive training and support to employees during the implementation phase. Offer tutorials, workshops, and documentation to help them understand the system's benefits. Encourage employees to ask questions and provide ongoing support as they familiarize themselves with the CRM tool.

2. **Cost of implementation and subscription**: Evaluate different CRM options and choose one that aligns with your budget and requirements. Consider both upfront costs and ongoing subscription fees. Additionally, assess the potential return on investment (ROI) by calculating the expected benefits and cost savings the CRM tool can provide your SMB.

3. **Integration challenges with existing systems**: Before implementing a CRM tool, assess its compatibility with your existing systems. Look for CRM solutions that offer seamless integration capabilities or provide APIs (Application Programming Interfaces) to connect with other essential business tools. Consult with IT professionals or CRM vendors for guidance on integration processes.

4. **Potential resistance from employees**: Communicate the benefits of implementing CRM tools to your employees. Clearly explain how the CRM tool can streamline their workflows, improve customer interactions, and enhance overall productivity. Involve employees in decision-making, listen to their concerns, and address them proactively. Offer incentives or rewards for employees who actively adopt and utilize the CRM tool.

5. **Data security and privacy concerns**: Choose a reputable CRM vendor prioritizing data security and compliance. Ensure the CRM tool complies with relevant data privacy regulations, such as GDPR (General Data Protection Regulation) or CCPA (California Consumer Privacy Act). To protect sensitive customer information, implement appropriate security measures, such as encryption, user access controls, and regular data backups.

By taking these steps, you can mitigate the potential challenges and maximize the benefits of implementing CRM tools for your SMB.

Here are some popular CRM tools for SMBs:

1. **Salesforce**: Salesforce is one of the leading CRM platforms offering a wide range of sales, marketing, and customer service features. It provides advanced customization options and integrates seamlessly with other business tools.

2. **HubSpot CRM**: HubSpot CRM is a free tool with robust contact management, lead tracking, and email automation features. It provides a user-friendly interface and integrates with HubSpot's marketing and sales tools.

3. **Zoho CRM**: Zoho CRM is a comprehensive CRM solution that caters to the needs of SMBs. It offers lead management,

sales forecasting, and social media integration features. Zoho CRM also provides integration capabilities with other Zoho applications.

4. **Pipedrive**: Pipedrive is a CRM tool designed specifically for sales teams. It provides a visual sales pipeline, email integration, and activity-tracking features. Pipedrive offers a user-friendly interface suitable for SMBs focused on sales management.

5. **Freshworks CRM**: Freshworks CRM (formerly Freshsales) is a cloud-based platform offering contact management, lead scoring, and deal management features. It provides a user-friendly interface and integrates with popular business tools.

6. **Insightly**: Insightly is a CRM tool that combines contact management, project management, and workflow automation features. It is suitable for SMBs requiring CRM functionalities and project management capabilities.

These are just a few examples of CRM tools available for SMBs. When choosing a CRM tool, consider your business requirements, budget, and integration needs to find the best fit for your SMB.

Setting up

To set up a CRM (Customer Relationship Management) system, follow these general steps:

1. **Define your CRM goals**: Determine what you want to achieve with your CRM system. Identify your business objectives, such as improving customer relationships, streamlining sales processes, or enhancing customer service.

2. **Evaluate CRM options**: Research and compare different CRM software options available in the market. Consider features, pricing, scalability, integration capabilities, and user-

friendliness. Choose a CRM solution that aligns with your business needs and budget.

3. **Plan your CRM implementation**: Create a detailed plan for implementing the CRM system. Define the scope of the implementation, establish a timeline, and allocate resources. Identify key stakeholders and assign responsibilities for each stage of the implementation process.

4. **Clean and import data**: Cleanse your existing customer data to ensure accuracy and consistency. Remove duplicate records, update outdated information, and standardize data formats. Then, import the cleaned data into the CRM system. Ensure that data fields in your CRM align with your business requirements.

5. **Configure CRM settings**: Customize the CRM system to match your business processes and workflows. Configure user roles and permissions, sales stages, and customer segmentation settings. Set up email templates, automation rules, and sales pipelines per your requirements.

6. **Integrate with other systems**: If necessary, integrate your CRM system with other essential business tools, such as email marketing platforms, e-commerce systems, or accounting software. This integration allows for seamless data flow between systems and improves overall efficiency.

7. **Train users**: Provide comprehensive training to your team members using the CRM system. Train them on navigating the CRM interface, entering and updating data, generating reports, and utilizing CRM features effectively. Offer ongoing support and resources, such as user manuals or video tutorials.

8. **Test and refine**: Conduct thorough testing of the CRM system to ensure its functionality and performance. Identify any issues or areas for improvement and make necessary adjustments.

Collect feedback from users and incorporate their suggestions to refine the system further.

9. **Roll out the CRM system**: Once you are confident in the system's readiness, launch the CRM system to your team. Communicate the benefits and importance of using the CRM system and encourage adoption. Monitor the system usage and address any concerns or questions from users.

10. **Continuous improvement**: Regularly review and evaluate the effectiveness of your CRM system. Analyze key performance metrics, gather user feedback, and identify improvement areas. Consider implementing updates, additional features, or integrations as your business needs evolve.

Remember that each CRM system may have specific setup instructions and requirements. Please consult the documentation and support resources provided by your chosen CRM software vendor for detailed guidance tailored to their system.

Predictive analytics and future forecasting

Predictive analytics and future forecasting can be powerful tools for small and medium-sized businesses (SMBs) to drive business growth. By leveraging historical data, market trends, and advanced statistical models, SMBs can make informed decisions and predictions about future outcomes.

Here are some ways SMBs can use predictive analytics and future forecasting for business growth:

1. **Demand Forecasting**: By analyzing historical data and market trends, SMBs can forecast customer demand for their products or services. This allows them to optimize inventory management, production planning, and resource allocation, ensuring they meet customer needs while minimizing costs.

2. **Customer Segmentation**: Predictive analytics can help SMBs identify customer segments based on their preferences, behaviors, and purchasing patterns. This enables targeted marketing campaigns, personalized offerings, and improved customer experiences, increasing customer satisfaction and loyalty.

3. **Churn Prediction**: SMBs can use predictive analytics to identify customers at risk of churning or ending their relationship with the business. By proactively targeting these

customers with retention strategies or personalized offers, SMBs can reduce churn rates and improve customer retention.

4. **Price Optimization:** Future forecasting can help SMBs optimize their pricing strategies by analyzing market dynamics, competitor pricing, and customer demand. By identifying price elasticity and understanding the impact of price changes, SMBs can set optimal prices that maximize revenue and profitability.

5. **Risk Assessment:** Predictive analytics can assist SMBs in assessing and managing risks associated with various business decisions. Whether evaluating credit risk, fraud detection, or identifying potential operational issues, predictive models can provide insights to mitigate risks and make more informed decisions.

It's important to note that while predictive analytics and future forecasting can provide valuable insights, they could be more foolproof. SMBs should continuously monitor and evaluate their models, validate predictions against actual outcomes, and adapt their strategies accordingly.

By harnessing the power of predictive analytics and future forecasting, SMBs can gain a competitive edge, drive business growth, and make data-driven decisions that contribute to long-term success.

Case Study: Improving Customer Retention

Company: XYZ Retail

XYZ Retail, a small retail business, faced customer retention challenges. They were losing many customers each month, impacting their revenue and profitability. To address this issue, they decided to leverage predictive analytics to identify customers at risk of churning and implement targeted retention strategies.

XYZ Retail built a predictive model to identify customers likely to churn using historical customer data, purchase history, and demographic information. The model considered factors such as frequency of purchases, average order value, and recent interactions with the business.

Once the model identified at-risk customers, XYZ Retail implemented a personalized retention strategy. They sent targeted emails offering exclusive discounts, rewards, and personalized recommendations based on individual preferences. They also assigned dedicated customer service representatives to reach out to at-risk customers and address their concerns.

The results were significant. XYZ Retail saw a noticeable reduction in customer churn rates. By proactively targeting at-risk customers and providing personalized offers, they were able to retain a higher percentage of customers and improve customer satisfaction.

Furthermore, by continuously monitoring and refining its predictive model, XYZ Retail was able to optimize its retention strategies over time. They identified new factors influencing customer churn and incorporated them into their model, improving accuracy.

The success of their customer retention efforts increased customer loyalty and positively impacted XYZ Retail's bottom line. They experienced a boost in revenue and profitability due to lower churn rates and increased customer lifetime value.

This case study highlights how predictive analytics can be a powerful tool for SMBs to improve customer retention and drive business growth. By leveraging data-driven insights, businesses can implement targeted strategies that address their customers' specific needs and preferences, ultimately leading to higher customer satisfaction and long-term success.

Implementation of Predictive analytics and future forecasting in SMB

To implement predictive analytics and future forecasting in their business, small and medium-sized enterprises (SMBs) can follow these step-by-step guidelines:

1. **Define Objectives**: Clearly define the objectives and goals of using predictive analytics and future forecasting in the business. Determine which areas of the company you want to improve or optimize, such as demand forecasting, customer segmentation, churn prediction, price optimization, or risk assessment.
2. **Data Collection**: Gather relevant data from various sources within your business, such as customer information, sales data, financial records, and market data. Ensure the data is accurate, complete, and properly structured for analysis.
3. **Data Preparation**: Cleanse and preprocess the collected data to remove errors, inconsistencies, and missing values. Transform and format the data into a suitable format for analysis. This may involve data normalization, feature engineering, and handling outliers.
4. **Data Analysis**: Apply statistical techniques, machine learning algorithms, and predictive modeling to analyze the prepared data. Use appropriate tools and software to identify patterns,

correlations, and trends that can provide insights into future outcomes.

5. **Model Development**: Develop predictive models based on the specific objectives of your business. Select appropriate algorithms for your data and purposes, such as regression, decision trees, or neural networks. Train the models using historical data and validate their performance using techniques like cross-validation.

6. **Implementation**: Implement the predictive models into your business operations. This may involve integrating the models into existing systems or developing new software applications that utilize the predictions and insights generated by the models.

7. **Monitoring and Evaluation**: Continuously monitor the performance of the predictive models and evaluate their accuracy and effectiveness. Compare the predicted outcomes with the actual results to assess the model's performance. Make necessary adjustments and refinements to improve the models over time.

8. **Actionable Insights**: Translate the predictions and insights generated by the models into actionable strategies and decisions. Use the forecasts to optimize inventory management, production planning, resource allocation, targeted marketing campaigns, personalized offerings, pricing strategies, risk mitigation, and customer retention strategies.

9. **Iterative Improvement**: Continuously improve and refine your models and strategies based on feedback and new data. Incorporate new variables, features, or data sources that can enhance the accuracy and relevance of your predictions. Stay updated with the latest research and advancements in

predictive analytics to improve your business's performance further.

By following these steps, SMBs can effectively implement predictive analytics and future forecasting in their business, driving growth, improving decision-making, and gaining a competitive advantage.

Challenges

Challenges in Implementing Predictive Analytics and Future Forecasting:

1. **Data Quality**: Poor data quality, such as missing values, inconsistencies, and errors, can affect the accuracy and reliability of predictive models. To overcome this challenge, SMBs should invest in data cleansing and preprocessing techniques, ensuring data accuracy and completeness before analysis.
2. **Data Availability**: More data is needed to develop robust predictive models. SMBs can address this challenge by leveraging external data sources or considering alternative data collection methods to supplement existing data.
3. **Expertise and Resources**: Implementing predictive analytics requires specialized knowledge and resources, including skilled data analysts, data scientists, and appropriate technology infrastructure. SMBs may overcome this challenge by partnering with external consultants or investing in training programs to build in-house capabilities.
4. **Model Interpretation**: Complex predictive models may be challenging to interpret and explain to stakeholders. SMBs should focus on developing interpretable models and provide

transparent explanations of the factors influencing predictions. This can help build trust and facilitate decision-making.

5. **Change Management**: Implementing predictive analytics may require organizational changes and a shift in decision-making processes. SMBs should communicate the benefits of predictive analytics to stakeholders, involve critical decision-makers from the start, and provide adequate support and training to ensure successful adoption.

6. **Ethical Considerations**: Predictive analytics can raise ethical concerns, such as data privacy, bias, and fairness. SMBs should prioritize ethical considerations throughout the implementation process, ensuring compliance with relevant regulations and guidelines.

Overcoming the Challenges:

1. **Start with Clear Objectives**: Clearly define the business objectives and ensure alignment between the predictive analytics initiative and the overall business strategy. This will provide a clear direction and help prioritize efforts.

2. **Invest in Data Governance**: Establish robust practices to ensure data quality, integrity, and security. Implement data validation processes, cleansing techniques, and regular monitoring to maintain data quality.

3. **Acquire and Leverage the Right Expertise**: Strengthen the team's expertise by hiring data analysts data scientists, or partnering with external consultants. Invest in training programs to enhance the analytical skills of existing team members.

4. **Choose the Right Tools and Technology**: Select appropriate tools and technologies that align with the business

requirements and scalability needs. Evaluate different software options and consider cloud-based solutions that offer flexibility and scalability.

5. **Iterative Approach**: Start with smaller projects and iterate over time. Begin with a simple predictive model and gradually incorporate complexity as the organization becomes more comfortable with the process. This approach allows for learning and refinement along the way.

6. **Collaboration and Communication**: Foster collaboration between data analysts, business users, and stakeholders. Encourage open communication channels to address concerns, share insights, and align expectations.

7. **Monitor and Evaluate**: Continuously monitor the performance of predictive models and evaluate their accuracy and effectiveness. Regularly review and refine the models based on new data and feedback.

8. **Ethical Considerations**: Prioritize ethical considerations in all stages of implementation. Establish policies and guidelines for data privacy, handle bias, and ensure fairness in predictive models. Involve legal and compliance teams to ensure compliance with regulations.

By proactively addressing these challenges and following best practices, SMBs can overcome implementation hurdles and successfully leverage predictive analytics and future forecasting to drive business growth and make informed decisions.

ENGAGING AND COLLABORATING WITH REMOTE TEAMS

Tools for remote work management

Tools for Remote Work Management

In today's digital age, remote work has become increasingly common, especially for small and medium-sized businesses (SMBs). To effectively manage remote teams and ensure productivity, SMBs can leverage various tools specifically designed for remote work management. These tools help streamline communication, collaboration, project management, and more. Here are some essential tools for remote work management:

1. Communication Tools

- **Video Conferencing**: Platforms like Zoom, Microsoft Teams, and Google Meet facilitate virtual face-to-face meetings, team discussions, and presentations.
- **Instant Messaging**: Tools like Slack, Microsoft Teams, and Discord enable real-time messaging, file sharing, and team collaboration.

2. Project Management Tools

- **Trello**: Trello is a popular project management tool that allows teams to manage tasks, assign responsibilities, track progress, and set deadlines.

- **Asana**: Asana provides a comprehensive platform for planning, organizing, and managing projects, including task management, team collaboration, and project tracking.

3. File Sharing and Collaboration Tools

- **Google Drive**: Google Drive offers cloud storage and file-sharing capabilities, allowing teams to collaborate on documents, spreadsheets, and presentations in real-time.
- **Microsoft OneDrive**: OneDrive is a cloud storage solution that integrates seamlessly with other Microsoft tools, enabling secure file sharing and collaboration.

4. Time Tracking and Productivity Tools

- **Toggl**: Toggl is a time-tracking tool that helps remote workers monitor their productivity, track time spent on tasks, and analyze work patterns.
- **RescueTime**: RescueTime provides insights into individual and team productivity by tracking time spent on applications, websites, and tasks.

These are just a few examples of the many tools available for remote work management. SMBs can choose the tools that best meet their needs and workflows, enabling seamless collaboration and efficient remote work operations.

How can Remote Work Management help enhance employee productivity

Remote work management tools can greatly improve employee productivity in several ways:

1. **Communication and Collaboration**: Remote work management tools provide efficient channels for communication and collaboration among team members. With real-time messaging, video conferencing, and file-sharing capabilities, employees can easily connect, share ideas, and collaborate on projects regardless of location. This improves team dynamics and allows for quick decision-making, increasing productivity.

2. **Task Management and Organization**: Remote work management tools offer task assignments, progress tracking, and deadline-setting features. These tools help employees stay organized and focused on tasks, ensuring everyone knows their responsibilities and deadlines. Employees can manage their time effectively and complete tasks promptly by having a clear overview of their jobs and priorities, boosting productivity.

3. **Access to Information and Resources**: Remote work management tools often provide centralized platforms for storing and accessing documents, files, and project-related information. This eliminates the need for lengthy email threads or searching through various folders to find the required information. Employees can quickly access the necessary resources, collaborate on documents in real time, and make informed decisions, increasing efficiency and productivity.

4. **Time Tracking and Optimization**: Many remote work management tools offer time-tracking features that allow employees to monitor the time spent on different tasks and projects. This helps identify productivity patterns, highlight improvement areas, and optimize work processes. By understanding how time is allocated, employees can adjust their work habits, eliminate time-wasting activities, and focus on high-value tasks, ultimately enhancing productivity.

5. **Employee Engagement and Well-being**: Remote work management tools often include features that promote employee engagement and well-being. These can consist of virtual team-building activities, employee recognition programs, and tools for monitoring and managing work-life balance. When employees feel supported and engaged, their motivation and productivity levels increase.

By utilizing remote work management tools effectively, organizations can overcome the challenges of remote work and create a productive and collaborative virtual work environment for their employees.

How to Decide which tools to use

When deciding which tools to use for remote work management, SMBs should consider several factors:

1. **Needs and Goals**: Assess the specific needs and goals of the company. Identify the critical challenges in remote work management and prioritize the features that address those challenges.
2. **Team Collaboration**: Consider how the tools facilitate effective team collaboration. Look for features like real-time messaging, file sharing, task assignment, and project tracking that promote seamless cooperation among team members.
3. **Integration**: Evaluate how well the tools integrate with existing systems and workflows. Consider tools that can integrate with the company's essential software, such as email clients, document editors, or project management platforms.
4. **User-Friendliness**: Choose tools that are intuitive and easy to use. Consider the learning curve for employees and ensure that

the means selected do not require extensive training or technical expertise.

5. **Scalability**: Consider the scalability of the tools. Determine if they can accommodate the company's growing needs as it expands and adapts to changing circumstances.

6. **Security**: Prioritize tools with robust security features, such as data encryption, access controls, and secure authentication methods. Ensure that the devices comply with relevant data protection and privacy regulations.

7. **Cost**: Consider the budget allocated for remote work management tools. Evaluate the pricing models of different devices, including subscription plans, licensing fees, or additional charges for advanced features.

By considering these factors, SMBs can make an informed decision about which tools to use for their company, ensuring that they align with their specific requirements and support efficient remote work operations.

Roadmap for Setting Up Remote Work Management

Setting up remote work management requires careful planning and implementation. Here is a roadmap to guide you through the process:

1. **Assess Your Needs**: Evaluate your organization's needs and goals for remote work management. Identify the key challenges and areas that need improvement. Consider factors such as communication, collaboration, project management, and productivity tracking.

2. **Research and Select Tools**: Conduct thorough research on remote work management tools available in the market. Consider each device's features, integrations, user-friendliness,

scalability, and security aspects. Shortlist the tools that best align with your organization's requirements.

3. **Pilot Test**: Conduct a pilot test with a small team or department before fully implementing a remote work management tool. This allows you to evaluate the tool's effectiveness and gather user feedback. Make any necessary adjustments or enhancements based on the pilot test results.

4. **Communicate and Train**: Communicate the purpose and benefits of remote work management to your employees. Provide training sessions or resources to familiarize them with the selected tools and their functionalities. Address any concerns or questions they may have during the training process.

5. **Establish Workflows and Guidelines**: Define transparent workflows and guidelines for remote work. This includes communication protocols, project management processes, and expectations for productivity and collaboration. Ensure that all team members understand and adhere to these guidelines.

6. **Implement the Tools**: Roll out your organization's selected remote work management tools. Set up user accounts, configure integrations with existing systems, and customize settings based on your organization's requirements. Provide ongoing support and assistance to employees during the implementation phase.

7. **Monitor and Evaluate**: Continuously monitor the usage and effectiveness of the remote work management tools. Gather feedback from employees and key stakeholders to identify areas for improvement. Regularly assess the impact of the devices on productivity, collaboration, and overall remote work operations.

8. **Iterate and Improve**: Based on feedback and evaluation, make necessary iterations and improvements to your remote work management strategies and tool implementation. Keep up with remote work's evolving needs and challenges, and adapt your approach accordingly.

9. **Promote Engagement and Well-being**: Foster employee engagement and well-being in a remote work environment. Implement initiatives such as virtual team-building activities, regular check-ins, and opportunities for recognition and feedback. Continuously assess and support the work-life balance of your employees.

10. **Stay Updated**: Stay informed about the latest trends, best practices, and advancements in remote work management. Regularly evaluate new tools and technologies to enhance your remote work operations.

By following this roadmap, you can effectively set up remote work management within your organization, promoting seamless communication, collaboration, and productivity among remote teams.

Case Study: Enhancing Remote Collaboration with XYZ Company

Client: XYZ Company, a global software development company with a distributed team across multiple countries.

Challenge: XYZ Company faced several challenges in effectively collaborating and managing their remote teams. The lack of a centralized communication platform resulted in disjointed communication channels, leading to miscommunication and delays in project delivery. The company also struggled to track project progress and ensure alignment among team members in different time zones. As a result, productivity and collaboration suffered.

Solution: XYZ Company implemented remote work management tools to address collaboration and productivity challenges. After thorough research, they selected a suite of tools, including a project management platform, a communication tool, and a time-tracking tool.

1. They implemented Asana as their project management platform, allowing teams to create and track tasks, set deadlines, and assign responsibilities. This provided a clear overview of project progress and ensured everyone knew their roles and responsibilities.
2. For communication, they adopted Slack as their primary tool. This allowed team members to communicate in real time, share files, and collaborate on projects. The integration of Slack with their project management tool enabled seamless communication within the context of specific tasks and projects.
3. To track time and monitor productivity, they utilized Toggl. This allowed employees to log their time on different tasks and projects, providing insights into individual and team productivity. The data from Toggl helped identify areas for improvement and optimize work processes.

Results: The implementation of remote work management tools brought significant improvements to XYZ Company's remote collaboration and productivity:

1. **Streamlined Communication:** Using Slack as a centralized communication platform improved team communication and

reduced the reliance on email. Real-time messaging, file sharing, and integration with project management tools facilitated seamless collaboration and quick decision-making.

2. **Enhanced Project Management:** Asana provided a comprehensive overview of project progress, ensuring that tasks were completed on time and team members remained aligned. The ability to assign responsibilities and set deadlines improved accountability and boosted productivity.

3. **Improved Productivity:** Using Toggl allowed employees to track their time and analyze their work patterns. This helped identify time-wasting activities and optimize work habits, increasing overall productivity. The data from Toggl also provided insights into resource allocation and workload distribution.

4. **Effective Remote Collaboration:** The combination of project management, communication, and time-tracking tools created a cohesive remote work environment. Team members could collaborate effectively regardless of physical location, improving collaboration and project outcomes.

Conclusion: By implementing remote work management tools, XYZ Company successfully addressed collaboration and productivity challenges. The streamlined communication, enhanced project management, and improved productivity resulted in a more efficient and collaborative remote work environment. The success of this case study highlights the importance of utilizing appropriate tools and technologies to support remote teams and ensure productive remote work operations.

Building a company culture in a digital workspace

Creating a Strong Foundation

Building a strong company culture in a digital workspace requires a solid foundation. This chapter will explore the key elements that contribute to a thriving company culture. We will discuss the importance of shared values, effective communication, and fostering collaboration among remote teams. Additionally, we will provide practical tips and strategies for creating a positive work environment in a virtual setting.

Stay tuned for the next chapter, where we will delve into the role of leadership in shaping company culture in a digital workspace.

Leadership plays a crucial role in shaping company culture in a digital workspace. Leaders are responsible for setting the tone and guiding the organization towards a positive and inclusive culture. They need to effectively communicate the company's values and goals and ensure that these are reflected in the actions and decisions of the team.

Leadership in a digital workspace fosters a sense of belonging and creates opportunities for remote team members to connect and collaborate. They should encourage open communication, provide support and resources, and promote a healthy work-life balance. Leaders can inspire and motivate employees by leading by example and actively engaging with the team, fostering a solid and cohesive company culture.

Additionally, leaders are responsible for promoting diversity and inclusion within the organization. They should actively seek diverse perspectives, value different ideas, and create an environment where everyone feels respected and included. By embracing diversity, leaders can cultivate a culture of innovation and creativity in a digital workspace.

Overall, leadership in a digital workspace plays a crucial role in shaping company culture by setting the correct values, fostering collaboration, promoting inclusivity, and inspiring and motivating the team.

Company leadership can achieve a strong company culture in a digital workspace by:

1. Setting clear values: Leadership should define and communicate the company's core values that align with the desired culture. These values should guide decision-making and behaviors within the organization.
2. Leading by example: Leaders should embody the desired culture and behavior themselves. They should demonstrate transparency, integrity, and inclusivity in their actions and interactions with employees.
3. Effective communication: Leaders should establish open lines of communication, both formal and informal, to ensure that employees feel heard and understood. Regularly sharing updates, providing feedback, and actively listening to employees' concerns and ideas are essential.
4. Fostering collaboration: Leadership should create opportunities for remote teams to collaborate effectively. This

can be done through virtual team-building activities, cross-functional projects, and platforms that facilitate communication and collaboration.

5. Promoting inclusivity: Leaders should actively encourage diversity and inclusion within the organization. This involves creating a safe and inclusive environment where different perspectives are valued and respected. Encouraging employee resource groups and implementing diversity and inclusion training programs can contribute to a more inclusive culture.

6. Providing support and resources: Leaders should ensure remote team members have the necessary resources, tools, and help to thrive in a digital workspace. This includes providing access to training, professional development opportunities, and technology infrastructure.

7. Recognizing and rewarding achievements: Leadership should acknowledge and celebrate the achievements and contributions of remote team members. This can be done through virtual recognition programs, rewards, and incentives.

By implementing these strategies, company leadership can foster a positive and inclusive company culture in a digital workspace, creating a sense of belonging, collaboration, and employee motivation.

Challenges and How to Overcome Them

While building a company culture in a digital workspace can be highly rewarding, there are some challenges that organizations may face. Here are a few possible challenges and strategies to overcome them:

1. **Lack of Face-to-Face Interaction**: In a digital workspace, the absence of in-person interaction can make building strong relationships challenging and foster a sense of connection. To

overcome this, leaders can encourage virtual social events, team-building activities, and informal video calls to promote personal relations among remote team members.

2. **Communication Breakdowns**: Effective communication is crucial for a thriving company culture. However, miscommunication and information gaps can occur in a digital workspace. To address this challenge, leaders should establish clear communication channels, encourage regular check-ins, and provide virtual meetings and collaboration guidelines.

3. **Maintaining Work-Life Balance**: Remote work can blur the boundaries between work and personal life, leading to burnout and decreased well-being. Leaders should actively support a healthy work-life balance by setting clear expectations, encouraging breaks, and promoting self-care practices among team members.

4. **Building Trust and Engagement**: Trust is essential for a strong company culture, but building trust in a digital workspace with limited face-to-face interactions can be challenging. Leaders can foster trust by promoting transparency, being accessible and responsive, and creating open dialogue and feedback opportunities.

5. **Managing Time Zones and Cultural Differences**: In a globally dispersed team, navigating different time zones and cultural norms can pose a challenge. Leaders should establish clear guidelines for scheduling meetings, foster cultural awareness and sensitivity, and ensure that all team members have equal opportunities for participation and contribution.

6. **Ensuring Inclusion and Diversity**: In a digital workspace, ensuring that all team members feel included and their diverse perspectives are valued can be challenging. Leaders should promote inclusivity by creating a safe and respectful

environment, addressing biases and microaggressions, and providing opportunities for diverse voices to be heard.

By addressing these challenges proactively and implementing strategies to overcome them, leaders can build a strong company culture in a digital workspace and create an environment where remote team members feel connected, engaged, and valued.

Implementing a solid company culture in a digital workspace can bring several benefits to the organization:

1. **Increased Employee Engagement and Satisfaction**: A positive company culture fosters employees' sense of belonging and engagement. Employees who feel connected to the organization and its values are more likely to be motivated, productive, and satisfied.
2. **Better Collaboration and Teamwork**: A strong company culture promotes collaboration and teamwork among remote teams. When employees have a shared understanding of the organization's goals and values, they are more likely to work together effectively, exchange ideas, and support one another.
3. **Enhanced Innovation and Creativity**: A positive work environment encourages employees to share their unique perspectives and ideas. By embracing diversity and inclusivity, a strong company culture fosters an environment where creativity and innovation can thrive, leading to new solutions and approaches.
4. **Improved Communication and Knowledge Sharing**: Clear communication channels and open lines of communication are essential components of a strong company culture. When employees feel comfortable expressing their thoughts and ideas,

knowledge sharing becomes more effective, leading to better decision-making and problem-solving.

5. **Attracting and Retaining Top Talent**: A strong company culture can be a differentiating factor in attracting and retaining top talent. When potential candidates see a positive and inclusive work environment, they are more likely to be attracted to the organization. Additionally, employees who feel valued and supported are more likely to stay with the company long-term.

6. **Positive Brand Reputation**: A company with a strong and positive culture is likelier to have a favorable brand reputation. This can attract customers, partners, and investors who align with the organization's values and mission.

7. **Adaptability and Resilience**: A strong company culture in a digital workspace can help the organization adapt to change and navigate challenging situations more effectively. When employees are aligned with the organization's values and have a strong sense of purpose, they are more resilient and better equipped to face uncertainties.

Building a strong company culture in a digital workspace can lead to numerous benefits, including increased employee engagement, improved collaboration, enhanced innovation, and a positive brand reputation. It creates an environment where employees feel valued, connected, and motivated, contributing to the overall success and growth of the organization.

CYBERSECURITY: SAFEGUARDING YOUR DIGITAL ASSETS

Understanding the importance of digital security

In today's digital age, the importance of digital security cannot be overstated. With the increasing reliance on technology for various aspects of our lives, it is crucial to understand the significance of protecting our digital assets and information. This chapter will delve into the key reasons why digital security is essential and provide insights into the potential risks and consequences of neglecting it.

Safeguarding Personal Data

Digital security plays a vital role in safeguarding our data. From financial information to confidential documents and sensitive communication, our digital devices and online accounts hold a wealth of personal data that needs to be protected from unauthorized access. Failure to secure this data can lead to identity theft, financial loss, and privacy breaches.

Protecting Against Cyber Threats

The digital landscape is fraught with various cyber threats, including malware, phishing attacks, and data breaches. Understanding the importance of digital security equips individuals and organizations with the knowledge and tools to protect themselves against these threats. Adequate security measures such as firewalls, antivirus software, and strong passwords can significantly reduce the risk of falling victim to cybercrime.

Preserving Online Reputation

Our online presence is an integral part of our identity in today's interconnected world. The security of our digital presence directly impacts our reputation. By understanding the importance of digital security, individuals can protect their online reputation by preventing unauthorized access to their social media accounts, avoiding sharing sensitive information publicly, and being cautious of online scams.

Ensuring Business Continuity

Digital security is crucial for businesses to ensure continuity and protect sensitive company data. A single security breach can have severe consequences, including financial loss, reputational damage, and legal implications. Understanding the importance of digital security enables organizations to implement robust security measures, conduct regular risk assessments, and educate employees on best practices, thus minimizing the risk of cyber incidents.

Contributing to a Safer Digital Environment

By understanding the importance of digital security and acting upon it, individuals and organizations contribute to creating a safer digital environment for everyone. Responsible digital behavior, such as using strong passwords, regularly updating software, and being cautious of suspicious emails and links, protects oneself and helps prevent the spread of cyber threats and malware.

In conclusion, understanding the importance of digital security is crucial in today's interconnected world. Safeguarding personal data, protecting against cyber threats, preserving online reputation, ensuring business continuity, and contributing to a safer digital environment are all key reasons why digital security should be a top priority for individuals and organizations.

Implementation

Implementing digital security in small and medium-sized businesses (SMBs) requires a comprehensive approach. Here are some steps that an SMB can take to enhance digital security:

1. Conduct a risk assessment: Identify the potential vulnerabilities and threats to your business's digital assets. Assess the impact and likelihood of these risks to prioritize security measures.
2. Develop a security policy: Create a clear and comprehensive digital security policy outlining guidelines and procedures for employees. This policy should cover password management, data handling, access controls, and incident response.
3. Provide employee training: Educate your employees about the importance of digital security and provide training on best practices. This should include recognizing phishing attempts, using strong passwords, and securely handling sensitive data.
4. Implement strong access controls: Limit access to sensitive data and systems only to authorized personnel. Use robust authentication methods such as multi-factor authentication to enhance security.
5. Regularly update software and systems: Keep all software, operating systems, and firmware up to date with the latest security patches. Periodically apply updates to address vulnerabilities and protect against known threats.

6. Backup and disaster recovery: Implement regular data backups and test the restoration process to ensure business continuity in case of data loss or security incidents.
7. Use encryption: Encrypt sensitive data at rest and in transit to protect it from unauthorized access. This includes encrypting data on devices, using secure communication protocols, and implementing secure file transfer methods.
8. Monitor and detect threats: Deploy security monitoring tools and techniques to detect and respond to potential security incidents. This can include intrusion detection systems, log monitoring, and real-time threat intelligence.
9. Regularly assess and improve security: Conduct periodic security assessments and audits to identify areas for improvement. Stay updated on the latest security trends and technologies to adapt your security measures accordingly.
10. Engage with security professionals: Consider partnering with external security experts or consultants to assess your security posture, provide recommendations, and assist in implementing robust security measures.

Remember, digital security is an ongoing process. It requires continuous monitoring, updating, and adaptation to stay ahead of evolving cyber threats. SMBs can mitigate risks and protect their valuable assets by prioritizing digital security.

Possible Threats

Some possible threats that a company needs to protect against include:

1. Malware: Malicious software designed to disrupt computer operations, steal data, or gain unauthorized access to systems.

2. Phishing: Attempts to deceive individuals into revealing sensitive information, such as passwords or credit card numbers, by impersonating a trustworthy entity.
3. Data breaches: Unauthorized access to sensitive data, leading to potential theft, exposure, or misuse of confidential information.
4. Ransomware: Malware that encrypts files or systems, demanding a ransom payment in exchange for restoring access.
5. Insider threats: Malicious or negligent actions by employees, contractors, or partners, potentially resulting in data breaches or other security incidents.
6. Social engineering: Manipulating individuals to disclose sensitive information or perform actions that compromise security.
7. Distributed Denial of Service (DDoS) attacks: Overwhelming a target's network or website with a flood of traffic, making it inaccessible to legitimate users.
8. Insider attacks: Deliberate misuse of authorized access privileges by individuals within the organization, leading to data breaches or other security incidents.
9. Physical theft or loss of devices: Unauthorized access to company devices or loss of physical devices containing sensitive information.
10. Advanced Persistent Threats (APTs): Sophisticated, targeted attacks by skilled adversaries, often aiming to gain persistent access to a network or system.

These are just a few examples of potential threats companies should be aware of and protect against.

Roadmap for Digital Security Implementation

1. **Phase 1: Assessment and Planning**
   - o Conduct a comprehensive risk assessment to identify potential vulnerabilities and threats.
   - o Evaluate the current digital security measures and identify areas for improvement.
   - o Set clear goals and objectives for enhancing digital security.

2. **Phase 2: Policy and Procedure Development**
   - o Develop a clear and comprehensive digital security policy.
   - o Define guidelines and procedures for employees to follow.
   - o Establish protocols for incident response and data handling.

3. **Phase 3: Employee Training and Awareness**
   - o Provide training sessions to educate employees about digital security best practices.
   - o Raise awareness about common threats like phishing, malware, and social engineering.
   - o Emphasize the importance of password management and safe data handling.

4. **Phase 4: Access Control and Authentication**
   - o Implement strong access controls and authentication methods.
   - o Limit access to sensitive data and systems to authorized personnel only.
   - o Utilize multi-factor authentication for enhanced security.

5. **Phase 5: Security Infrastructure Enhancement**

- o   Regularly update software, operating systems, and firmware with the latest security patches.
- o   Implement encryption protocols for data at rest and in transit.
- o   Deploy security monitoring tools to detect and respond to potential incidents.

6. **Phase 6: Backup and Disaster Recovery**
- o   Establish a regular backup schedule for critical data.
- o   Test the restoration process to ensure data can be recovered effectively.
- o   Develop a comprehensive disaster recovery plan to minimize downtime.

7. **Phase 7: Ongoing Monitoring and Improvement**
- o   Continuously monitor the digital security landscape for emerging threats.
- o   Conduct periodic security assessments and audits.
- o   Stay updated on the latest security trends and technologies.

8. **Phase 8: External Collaboration and Expertise**
- o   Engage with external security professionals or consultants for guidance and support.
- o   Seek third-party assessments to validate the effectiveness of security measures.
- o   Collaborate with industry peers to share best practices and insights.

Remember, this roadmap is a general guide and can be adapted based on your organization's specific needs and resources. Regularly reassess and update your digital security strategy to stay ahead of evolving threats.

Case Study: XYZ Company's Digital Security Transformation

Situation

XYZ Company, a medium-sized technology firm, recognized the increasing importance of digital security in safeguarding their valuable assets and protecting their clients' data. They wanted to enhance their digital security measures to mitigate potential risks and ensure compliance with industry regulations.

Challenges

- We have limited awareness and understanding of emerging cyber threats among employees.
- Outdated security policies and procedures that did not align with current best practices.
- Insufficient access controls and authentication methods to protect sensitive data.
- Inadequate disaster recovery plan and backup processes.
- Lack of regular security assessments and monitoring mechanisms.

Approach

XYZ Company embarked on a comprehensive digital security transformation journey to address these challenges and improve its overall security posture. The following steps were taken:

1. **Awareness and Training**: Company-wide training sessions were conducted to educate employees about best digital security practices. Employees were trained to recognize

phishing attempts, use strong passwords, and identify potential security risks.

2. **Policy and Procedure Update**: Revised and updated the digital security policy to align with current industry standards and regulatory requirements. Clear guidelines and procedures were established for data handling, incident response, and access controls.

3. **Access Control Enhancement**: Implemented multi-factor authentication for all critical systems and restricted access to sensitive data based on job roles and responsibilities. Regular access reviews were conducted to ensure only authorized personnel had access.

4. **Infrastructure Upgrade**: Upgraded software, operating systems, and firmware with the latest security patches. Encryption protocols were implemented for data at rest and in transit. Security monitoring tools were deployed to detect and respond to potential security incidents.

5. **Backup and Disaster Recovery**: Developed a comprehensive backup strategy to back up critical data regularly and tested the restoration process to ensure data recoverability. A robust disaster recovery plan was created to minimize downtime in case of a security incident.

6. **Security Assessments and Audits**: Conducted periodic security assessments and audits to identify vulnerabilities and areas for improvement. External security experts were engaged to perform penetration testing and recommend further enhancements.

7. **Continuous Improvement**: Established a culture of constant improvement by staying updated on the latest security trends and technologies. Regular security awareness campaigns and

refresher training sessions were conducted to reinforce digital security practices.

Results

- Increased employee awareness and understanding of digital security risks, leading to a proactive approach to security.
- Enhanced access controls and authentication methods, ensuring only authorized personnel could access sensitive data.
- Improved compliance with regulatory requirements and industry standards.
- It strengthened disaster recovery and backup processes, minimizing downtime and data loss in case of a security incident.
- Regular security assessments and audits helped identify and address vulnerabilities before they could be exploited.
- External collaboration with security experts provided valuable insights and guidance for ongoing security improvements.

XYZ Company's digital security transformation improved its ability to protect valuable assets and sensitive data and instilled confidence among its clients and partners. By prioritizing digital security, they demonstrated their commitment to maintaining a secure and trustworthy environment for their stakeholders.

Best practices to secure business data

Protecting business data is crucial for maintaining the security and integrity of an organization. Here are some best practices to ensure the safety of your business data:

1. Implement Strong Password Policies:
   - Encourage employees to use unique and complex passwords.
   - Enforce regular password updates.
   - Implement multi-factor authentication whenever possible.
2. Regularly Update Software and Systems:
   - Keep all software and operating systems up to date with the latest security patches.
   - Enable automatic updates whenever possible.
3. Use Encryption:
   - Encrypt sensitive data at rest and in transit to prevent unauthorized access.
   - Implement secure encryption protocols for communication channels.
4. Implement Access Controls:
   - Grant access privileges based on the principle of least privilege.

- o Regularly review and update user access rights to ensure appropriate access levels.

5. Provide Security Awareness Training:
   - o Educate employees about data security best practices.
   - o Train them on identifying and reporting potential security threats.

6. Backup Data Regularly:
   - o Implement automated backup solutions to ensure regular and secure backups.
   - o Test data restoration processes periodically to ensure data integrity.

7. Monitor and Audit:
   - o Implement robust monitoring and logging systems to detect and respond to security incidents.
   - o Regularly review audit logs to identify potential security breaches.

Remember, securing business data is an ongoing process. Regularly reassess and update your security measures to adapt to evolving threats and technologies.

TECH-DRIVEN CUSTOMER SERVICE

Chatbots and automated support

Chatbots and automated support systems offer numerous advantages for small and medium-sized businesses (SMBs). By implementing these technologies, SMBs can experience the following benefits:

1. Improved Customer Service

Chatbots provide instant responses to customer inquiries, offering 24/7 support. This enhances customer satisfaction by reducing response times and ensuring prompt assistance. Automated support systems can handle many customer interactions simultaneously, ensuring no customer is left waiting.

2. Cost Savings

Implementing chatbots and automated support systems can significantly reduce operational costs. Businesses can optimize their resources and allocate human support agents to more complex or specialized tasks by automating repetitive tasks and providing self-service options. This reduces the need for a large customer support team, resulting in cost savings.

3. Increased Efficiency

Chatbots and automated support systems are designed to handle multiple tasks simultaneously, allowing businesses to run more customer inquiries efficiently. By automating routine tasks, such as providing essential information or processing simple transactions, employees can focus on more critical tasks that require human expertise.

4. Personalized Customer Experience

With advanced machine learning capabilities, chatbots can analyze customer data and provide personalized recommendations or responses. They can remember customer preferences, previous interactions, and purchase history, allowing for tailored and relevant interactions. This customized experience builds customer loyalty and enhances the overall brand perception.

5. Scalability

As businesses grow, so does the demand for customer support. Chatbots and automated support systems offer scalability, as they can handle increasing customer inquiries without additional resources. This ensures that customer service remains efficient and effective, even during periods of high demand.

In conclusion, implementing chatbots and automated support systems can provide numerous benefits for SMBs, including improved customer service, cost savings, increased efficiency, personalized customer experiences, and scalability. These technologies empower businesses to deliver exceptional customer support while optimizing resources and driving growth.

Implementation

To implement chatbots and automated support systems in an SMB, the following steps can be taken:

1. Identify Use Cases: Determine where chatbots and automated support can benefit the business. This could include customer inquiries, order processing, appointment scheduling, or FAQs.

2. Choose the Right Platform: Research a suitable chatbot or automated support system that aligns with the business's requirements and budget. Consider factors such as ease of implementation, integration capabilities, customization options, and scalability.

3. Design and Development: Define the chatbot's functionality, conversational flow, and user experience. Work with developers or utilize no-code/low-code platforms to build and customize the chatbot based on the identified use cases. Test the chatbot thoroughly to ensure it meets the desired requirements.

4. Integration: Integrate the chatbot or automated support system with existing business systems, such as CRM, ticketing systems, or knowledge bases. This enables seamless data exchange and provides a holistic view of customer interactions.

5. Training and Maintenance: Train employees who manage or interact with the chatbot. Continuously monitor and analyze the chatbot's performance to identify areas for improvement. Update and refine the chatbot's responses based on user feedback and evolving business needs.

6. Customer Feedback and Iteration: Encourage customers to provide feedback on their interactions with the chatbot. Use this feedback to refine and optimize the chatbot's responses, improve accuracy, and enhance the overall customer experience.

Following these steps, SMBs can implement chatbots and automated support systems to enhance customer service, streamline operations, and drive business growth.

Challenges and Solutions

Implementing chatbots and automated support systems may come with specific challenges. Here are some potential challenges and ways to overcome them:

1. **Initial Development and Training**: Developing and training a chatbot or automated support system requires time, resources, and expertise. To overcome this challenge, businesses can consider collaborating with chatbot development experts or utilizing no-code/low-code platforms that simplify development.

2. **Data Integration and System Compatibility**: Integrating the chatbot or automated support system with existing business systems may pose compatibility issues. To address this challenge, thorough testing and validation should be conducted during the integration phase. It may also be beneficial to seek support from IT professionals or software developers to ensure seamless data exchange.

3. **Natural Language Understanding**: Ensuring the chatbot understands and responds accurately to a wide range of user queries can be challenging. To overcome this, machine learning and natural language processing techniques can be employed to train and improve the chatbot's language understanding capabilities continuously.

4. **User Acceptance and Trust**: Some users may be skeptical or resist interacting with chatbots. Businesses can provide clear information about the chatbot's capabilities and limitations to foster user acceptance and build trust. Additionally, offering a seamless transition to human support when necessary can help reassure customers.

5. **Ongoing Maintenance and Updates**: Chatbots and automated support systems require constant maintenance and updates to keep up with evolving customer needs and technological advancements. To address this challenge, businesses should establish a dedicated team or assign responsible individuals to monitor the chatbot's performance, gather user feedback, and make necessary improvements.

By being aware of these potential challenges and implementing the suggested solutions, businesses can overcome obstacles and maximize the benefits of chatbots and automated support systems.

Some things to keep in mind

Before implementing chatbots and automated support systems, there are several key considerations to keep in mind:

1. **Define Clear Objectives**: Clearly define the goals and objectives you want to achieve with chatbot implementation. Determine how the technology will align with your business strategy and how it will benefit your customers and internal processes.
2. **Understand User Needs**: Conduct thorough research to understand your customers' preferences, pain points, and expectations. Identify the areas where chatbots and automated support systems can provide the most value and effectively address customer needs.
3. **Plan for Seamless Integration**: Evaluate your existing systems and infrastructure to ensure a smooth integration process. Determine how the chatbot will interact with other methods, such as CRM or ticketing systems, to provide a seamless customer experience.

4. **Consider Scalability**: Anticipate future growth and scalability needs when selecting a chatbot platform or automated support system. Ensure the chosen solution can handle increasing customer inquiries and adapt to evolving business requirements.

5. **Balance Automation and Human Touch**: Find the right balance between automation and human interaction. While chatbots can handle routine tasks, there may be situations where customers require human assistance. Plan for a seamless handoff between chatbots and human agents to provide personalized support when needed.

6. **Ensure Data Privacy and Security**: Implement robust security measures to protect customer data and ensure compliance with data privacy regulations. Choose a chatbot platform or automated support system prioritizing data encryption, secure data storage, and user consent mechanisms.

7. **Test and Iterate**: Thoroughly test the chatbot before deployment to identify any issues or areas for improvement. Continuously gather user feedback and make iterative improvements to enhance the chatbot's performance and user experience.

8. **Provide Adequate Training**: Train your support team and employees who will interact with the chatbot to ensure they understand its capabilities, limitations, and how to handle complex or escalated customer inquiries.

9. **Monitor Performance and Metrics**: Establish key performance indicators (KPIs) to measure the success and effectiveness of the chatbot. Regularly monitor and analyze performance metrics to identify areas for optimization and make data-driven decisions.

10. **Continuous Improvement**: Chatbots and automated support systems should be considered evolving technologies. Stay updated with industry trends and advancements to leverage new features and capabilities to enhance the chatbot's performance and improve customer experience.

By considering these factors and addressing them during the planning and implementation stages, you can maximize the benefits of chatbots and automated support systems while ensuring a successful integration into your business operations.

Case Study: Chatbot Implementation at XYZ Company

Objective

XYZ Company, a leading e-commerce platform, aimed to enhance its customer support capabilities and streamline the handling of customer inquiries. They sought to implement a chatbot solution to provide instant responses, improve efficiency, and deliver personalized customer experiences.

Implementation

1. **Identifying Use Cases**: XYZ Company recognized common customer inquiries, such as order tracking, product information, and returns/exchanges, as critical areas where a chatbot could add value.
2. **Choosing the Right Platform**: After thorough research, XYZ Company selected a chatbot platform that offered robust integration capabilities, natural language understanding, and scalability to meet its growing customer base.

3. **Design and Development**: XYZ Company collaborated with the chatbot platform provider to define the chatbot's conversational flow, develop responses, and integrate it with its existing systems, including CRM and order management.
4. **Integration**: The chatbot was seamlessly integrated into XYZ Company's website and mobile app, enabling customers to access support anytime, anywhere.
5. **Training and Maintenance**: The customer support team received comprehensive training on managing the chatbot and handling complex queries that required human intervention. The chatbot's performance was continuously monitored, and updates were made based on user feedback and evolving customer needs.

Results and Benefits

1. **Improved Customer Satisfaction**: The chatbot provided instant responses, reducing customer wait times and ensuring prompt assistance. Customers appreciated the 24/7 availability and personalized support, resulting in increased satisfaction.
2. **Efficiency and Cost Savings**: The chatbot handled many customer inquiries, allowing human support agents to focus on more complex tasks: this optimized resource allocation and reduced operational costs.
3. **Personalized Recommendations**: With advanced machine learning capabilities, the chatbot analyzed customer preferences and browsing history to provide tailored product recommendations, enhancing the customer shopping experience.
4. **Scalability and Growth**: As XYZ Company experienced growth, the chatbot seamlessly scaled to handle increasing

customer inquiries, ensuring efficient support during peak periods.

5. **Positive Brand Perception**: The chatbot implementation showcased XYZ Company's commitment to innovation and customer-centricity, enhancing its brand reputation.

Conclusion

By implementing a chatbot solution, XYZ Company successfully streamlined its customer support operations, improved efficiency, and delivered personalized customer experiences. The chatbot's 24/7 availability, instant responses, and ability to handle a high volume of inquiries resulted in higher customer satisfaction and cost savings. The case study highlights the benefits of chatbot implementation for enhancing customer support in the e-commerce industry.

Utilizing AI for enhanced customer interactions

Small and medium-sized businesses (SMBs) can benefit from utilizing AI for enhanced customer interactions in several ways:

1. **Improved customer service:** AI-powered chatbots and virtual assistants can respond instantly to customer inquiries, resolving issues quickly and efficiently.
2. **Personalized experiences:** AI algorithms can analyze customer data to understand preferences and behaviors, allowing SMBs to deliver customized recommendations and offers tailored to individual customers.
3. **24/7 availability:** AI-powered automation enables SMBs to provide round-the-clock customer support, ensuring customer inquiries are addressed outside regular business hours.
4. **Efficient customer feedback analysis:** AI tools can analyze customer feedback from various sources, such as surveys and social media, to identify trends and insights, helping SMBs make data-driven decisions to improve their products or services.
5. **Increased sales and revenue:** AI algorithms can analyze customer data and patterns to identify cross-selling and upselling opportunities, enabling SMBs to increase sales and revenue.

By leveraging AI for enhanced customer interactions, SMBs can improve customer satisfaction, streamline operations, and drive business growth.

Roadmap for AI Implementation

1. **Phase 1: Research and Planning**
   - Conduct a thorough assessment of the business's customer interactions and pain points.
   - Identify specific areas where AI can be implemented to enhance customer interactions.
   - Research and evaluate AI solutions and vendors that align with the business's needs and budget.
2. **Phase 2: Data Collection and Preparation**
   - Gather relevant customer data from various sources, such as CRM systems, customer support logs, and website analytics.
   - Clean and organize the data to ensure its quality and compatibility with AI algorithms.
   - Define key performance indicators (KPIs) to measure the success of AI implementation.
3. **Phase 3: AI Model Development**
   - Collaborate with AI experts and developers to build and train AI models tailored to the business's needs.
   - Implement AI-powered chatbots and virtual assistants to provide instant customer support and personalized experiences.
   - Test and refine the AI models to ensure accuracy and efficiency.

4. **Phase 4: Integration and Deployment**
   - Integrate the AI solutions into existing customer interaction channels, such as websites, mobile apps, and social media platforms.
   - Conduct thorough testing to ensure seamless integration and functionality.
   - Develop a strategy for monitoring and managing AI-powered customer interactions.

5. **Phase 5: Continuous Improvement**
   - Regularly analyze and evaluate the performance of AI-powered customer interactions using the defined KPIs.
   - Collect feedback from customers and employees to identify areas for improvement.
   - Iterate and enhance the AI models based on insights and feedback.

By following this roadmap, SMBs can successfully implement AI for enhanced customer interactions and unlock the numerous benefits it offers.

Tools

To implement AI-powered customer interactions, small and medium-sized businesses (SMBs) can explore the following tools:

1. **Chatbot platforms:** Chatfuel, ManyChat, and Dialogflow offer user-friendly interfaces to build and deploy AI-powered chatbots for customer support and engagement.
2. **Virtual assistant software:** Tools like IBM Watson Assistant, Microsoft Azure Virtual Assistant, and Amazon Lex enable SMBs to create virtual assistants that can handle customer inquiries and provide personalized recommendations.

3. **Customer relationship management (CRM) systems:** CRM systems like Salesforce, HubSpot, and Zoho CRM often include AI features that can enhance customer interactions, such as predictive analytics and AI-powered chatbots.
4. **Sentiment analysis tools:** Tools like MonkeyLearn, Lexalytics, and Brandwatch help SMBs analyze customer feedback from various sources to understand sentiment and make data-driven decisions.
5. **Recommendation engines:** Platforms like RichRelevance, Barilliance, and Dynamic Yield use AI algorithms to provide personalized product recommendations based on customer behavior and preferences.
6. **Voice assistants:** Integrating voice assistants like Amazon Alexa, Google Assistant, or Apple Siri into customer interaction channels allows SMBs to offer voice-enabled customer support and engagement.
7. **Social media listening tools:** Tools like Hootsuite, Sprout Social, and Mention enable SMBs to monitor and analyze customer conversations on social media, providing insights for improved customer interactions.

These tools offer SMBs a range of options to implement AI-powered customer interactions based on their specific needs and resources.

Threats & Solutions

Some possible threats that companies may need to protect against when implementing AI-powered customer interactions include:

1. **Data privacy and security:** AI implementation involves collecting and analyzing large amounts of customer data. Companies must ensure proper security measures are in place

to protect customer information from unauthorized access, breaches, and misuse.

2. **Bias and fairness:** AI algorithms can inadvertently perpetuate biases if the training data is biased or if the algorithms are not properly designed and tested. Companies must carefully monitor and address any preferences in AI models to ensure fair and equitable customer interactions.

3. **Customer trust and acceptance:** Some customers may be concerned about interacting with AI-powered systems. Companies need to address these concerns and ensure transparent communication to build customer trust and acceptance.

4. **Technical limitations and errors:** AI systems are imperfect and can make errors or provide inaccurate responses. Companies need to have processes to handle and rectify errors promptly and effectively to maintain a positive customer experience.

5. **Ethical considerations:** AI implementation raises ethical concerns, such as the responsible use of customer data, transparency in AI decision-making, and ensuring that AI systems do not infringe upon customer rights or discriminate against specific individuals or groups.

By proactively addressing these threats, companies can mitigate potential risks and ensure that AI-powered customer interactions are implemented responsibly and beneficially.

Case Study: AI-Enhanced Customer Interactions in E-commerce

Company Name: XYZ Electronics

Overview: XYZ Electronics, a leading e-commerce company specializing in consumer electronics, implemented AI-powered interactions to enhance customer satisfaction and drive sales. By leveraging AI technology, they were able to provide personalized experiences, improve customer service, and increase revenue.

Implementation:

1. **Personalized Product Recommendations:**
   - XYZ Electronics utilized a recommendation engine powered by AI algorithms to provide personalized product recommendations to customers based on their browsing and purchase history.
   - The system generated tailored recommendations by analyzing customer behavior and preferences, resulting in higher customer engagement and increased sales.
2. **AI-Powered Chatbot for Customer Support:**
   - XYZ Electronics deployed an AI-powered chatbot to handle customer inquiries and provide instant support.
   - The chatbot utilized natural language processing (NLP) algorithms to understand customer queries and provide relevant and timely responses.
   - Customers could get quick answers to their questions, improving customer satisfaction and reducing support costs.

3. **24/7 Customer Support:**
   - With the help of AI automation, XYZ Electronics extended its customer support availability to 24/7.
   - Customers could contact for assistance anytime, even outside regular business hours, ensuring their inquiries were addressed promptly.

Results:

1. **Increased Customer Engagement:**
   - The personalized product recommendations significantly improved customer engagement and conversion rates.
   - Customers appreciated the tailored suggestions, leading to higher customer satisfaction and repeat purchases.
2. **Improved Customer Service Efficiency:**
   - The AI-powered chatbot handled many customer inquiries, reducing the workload on human customer support agents.
   - This resulted in faster response times and improved efficiency in resolving customer issues.
3. **Revenue Growth:**
   - Combining personalized product recommendations, enhanced customer service, and round-the-clock availability led to a substantial increase in sales and revenue.
   - Customers felt valued and supported throughout their shopping journey, increasing customer loyalty and repeat business.

Conclusion:

By implementing AI-powered customer interactions, XYZ Electronics successfully enhanced customer satisfaction, streamlined customer service, and experienced significant business growth. The personalized experiences and efficient support AI technology provided were crucial in driving customer engagement and boosting sales. The XYZ Electronics case demonstrates AI's immense potential in revolutionizing customer interactions in the e-commerce industry.

Importance of timely and efficient customer support

Customer support plays a crucial role in the success of any business. Timely and efficient customer support can significantly impact customer satisfaction, loyalty, and overall business reputation. Here are several reasons why timely and efficient customer support is essential:

1. Customer Satisfaction

Timely and efficient customer support ensures customer issues and concerns are addressed promptly. When customers receive quick and practical support, they feel valued and appreciated. This leads to higher customer satisfaction and a positive perception of the company.

The Key to Customer Satisfaction: Timely and Efficient Support

Customer satisfaction is the cornerstone of a successful business. Companies must prioritize timely and efficient customer support to meet and exceed customer expectations. By providing quick and effective resolutions to customer issues, companies can foster a positive relationship with their customers and build a strong foundation for long-term success.

Promptly Addressing Customer Concerns

One of the main reasons why timely and efficient customer support is essential for customer satisfaction is that it ensures prompt resolution of customer concerns. When customers reach out for help, they want their issues to be acknowledged and addressed promptly. By promptly responding to customer inquiries and providing solutions, companies demonstrate their commitment to customer satisfaction.

Making Customers Feel Valued

Timely and efficient customer support also plays a significant role in making customers feel valued and appreciated. When customers receive quick and practical support, they think their concerns matter, and the company genuinely cares about their satisfaction. This positive experience resolves their immediate issues and strengthens their emotional connection with the brand.

Enhancing Customer Perception

How companies handle customer support can significantly influence how customers perceive the brand. When customers experience timely and efficient support creates a positive perception of the company as customer-centric and reliable. This positive word-of-mouth can spread among potential customers, further enhancing the company's reputation and attracting new business.

Building Customer Loyalty

Customer loyalty is built on a foundation of excellent customer support. When customers receive timely and efficient resolutions to their problems, they are likelier to remain loyal to the company. Satisfied customers not only continue using the products or services offered but also become advocates for the brand. Their positive experiences and recommendations contribute to increased customer loyalty and potential growth.

Gaining a Competitive Edge

In today's competitive business landscape, standing out is essential. Timely and efficient customer support can be a key differentiating factor. Companies that provide exceptional support gain a competitive edge over their rivals. Customers are likelier to choose a company that offers reliable and responsive support, as it instills confidence and trust in the brand.

Retaining Valuable Customers

Customer retention is crucial for long-term business success. Timely and efficient customer support plays a vital role in retaining valuable customers. Customers expect a prompt and satisfactory resolution when they encounter issues or have questions. By prioritizing timely support, companies can prevent customer churn and ensure that their customers remain loyal.

In conclusion, timely and efficient customer support is paramount for achieving high levels of customer satisfaction. It resolves customer issues promptly and makes customers feel valued, enhances brand perception, builds loyalty, and provides a competitive advantage. By investing in a robust customer support system and delivering exceptional service, companies can cultivate a loyal customer base and thrive in today's competitive market.

2. Customer Loyalty

Providing timely and efficient customer support builds customer loyalty. When customers experience efficient resolution of their problems, they are more likely to continue using the products or services offered by the company. Satisfied customers are also more likely to recommend the company to others, contributing to increased customer loyalty and potential growth.

The Power of Customer Loyalty

Customer loyalty is a valuable asset for any business. It goes beyond simply having repeat customers; it represents a deep connection and trust between the customer and the brand. Building customer loyalty is essential for long-term success in today's competitive market. Explore why customer loyalty is so important and how businesses can cultivate it.

The Benefits of Customer Loyalty

1. **Repeat Business**: Loyal customers are likelier to continue purchasing from a brand. They have already experienced the value and quality of the products or services and trust the brand to meet their needs consistently. This repeat business provides a stable revenue stream and contributes to the company's financial stability.

2. **Positive Word-of-mouth**: Loyal customers often become brand advocates, sharing their positive experiences with others. They recommend the brand to friends, family, and colleagues, effectively becoming a free marketing force. Positive word-of-mouth is incredibly powerful and can attract new customers who trust the recommendations of their peers.

3. **Increased Customer Lifetime Value**: Loyal customers tend to have higher lifetime value (CLV). They make repeat purchases and are more likely to try new products or services the brand offers. Their loyalty translates into higher average order values and a longer overall relationship with the company.

4. **Cost Savings**: Acquiring new customers can be expensive, requiring extensive marketing efforts. On the other hand, retaining existing customers is generally more cost-effective. By focusing on building customer loyalty, businesses can reduce customer acquisition costs and allocate resources more efficiently.

5. **Competitive Advantage**: Customer loyalty can be a key differentiating factor in a crowded marketplace. Businesses that prioritize building solid relationships with their customers gain a competitive edge. Customers are more likely to choose a brand they trust and have had positive experiences with, even if competitors offer similar offerings.

Cultivating Customer Loyalty

Now that we understand the importance of customer loyalty let's explore some strategies to cultivate and strengthen it:

1. Exceptional Customer Service

Providing exceptional customer service is the foundation of building loyalty. Customers want to feel valued and heard, especially when encountering issues or questions. Businesses can demonstrate their commitment to customer satisfaction and build trust by prioritizing timely and efficient customer support.

2. Personalized Experiences

Tailoring experiences to individual customers can make them feel special and appreciated. This can include personalized recommendations, exclusive offers, or even a simple personalized thank-you note. Businesses can forge a deeper connection and foster loyalty by showing genuine interest in the customer's preferences and needs.

3. Loyalty Programs

Implementing a loyalty program is an effective way to reward and incentivize repeat customers. Whether through points, discounts, or exclusive perks, loyalty programs make customers feel appreciated and encourage them to continue choosing the brand over competitors.

4. Consistent Communication

Maintaining regular and meaningful communication with customers is crucial for building loyalty. This can be through email newsletters, social media updates, or personalized follow-ups. By staying top-of-mind and providing valuable information, businesses can nurture the relationship and reinforce loyalty.

5. Continuous Improvement

Listening to customer feedback and continuously improving products, services, and processes is vital for maintaining loyalty. Customers appreciate when their opinions are valued and see that the brand is actively working to meet their evolving needs. By staying agile and responsive, businesses can adapt to changing customer expectations and strengthen loyalty.

The Bottom Line

Customer loyalty is a powerful force that drives business success. It leads to repeat business, positive word-of-mouth, and increased customer lifetime value. Companies can cultivate strong customer loyalty by prioritizing exceptional customer service, personalizing experiences, implementing loyalty programs, maintaining consistent communication, and continuously improving. Investing in building loyalty is an investment in the long-term growth and sustainability of the company.

Remember, loyal customers are not just customers but brand advocates and partners on the journey to success.

3. Brand Reputation

A company's reputation is closely tied to its customer support. Customers receiving timely and efficient support enhances the company's reputation as a customer-centric organization. Positive word-of-mouth spreads, attracting new customers and fostering trust in the brand. On the other hand, poor customer support can lead to negative reviews and damage the company's reputation.

The Power of Brand Reputation

A company's brand reputation is a valuable asset that can significantly impact its success in the marketplace. It is the perception that customers, stakeholders, and the public have of a brand based on their experiences, interactions, and the company's overall image. A strong brand reputation can be a powerful tool, attracting customers, building trust, and providing a competitive edge. On the other hand, a poor brand reputation can lead to lost opportunities, decreased customer loyalty, and a tarnished image.

The Importance of a Positive Brand Reputation

1. **Building Trust**: A positive brand reputation builds trust with customers. When customers have confidence in a brand, they are more likely to choose its products or services over competitors. Trust is the foundation of successful customer relationships, and a positive reputation helps establish that trust.

2. **Customer Loyalty**: A strong brand reputation fosters customer loyalty. Customers who have had positive experiences with a brand are more likely to remain loyal and continue supporting the company. They become brand advocates, recommending the brand to others and contributing to its growth.

3. **Attracting Customers**: A positive brand reputation attracts new customers. When potential customers see a brand has a good reputation, they are likelier to choose it over other options. Positive word-of-mouth and online reviews play a significant role in attracting new customers and expanding the customer base.

4. **Competitive Advantage**: A strong brand reputation provides a competitive advantage in the market. Customers are more likely to choose a brand they trust and have heard positive things about, even if competitors offer similar offerings. A positive reputation sets a brand apart from the competition and can be a key differentiating factor.

5. **Crisis Resilience**: Companies with a positive brand reputation are more resilient in times of crisis. When a brand has built a strong trust and loyalty foundation, it is better equipped to

weather adverse events or challenges. Customers are more likely to give the benefit of the doubt and continue supporting the brand through difficult times.

Building and Maintaining a Positive Brand Reputation

Building and maintaining a positive brand reputation requires a proactive approach and ongoing efforts. Here are some strategies to consider:

1. **Consistent Brand Messaging**: Ensure your brand messaging is consistent across all channels and touchpoints. This includes advertising, social media, customer interactions, and other communication. Consistency helps build trust and reinforces the brand's identity.

2. **Exceptional Customer Experience**: A unique customer experience is critical to building a positive brand reputation. Focus on delivering outstanding products or services, personalized interactions, and prompt customer support. Strive to exceed customer expectations at every opportunity.

3. **Transparency and Authenticity**: Be transparent in your business practices and communicate openly with customers. Authenticity builds trust and helps establish a genuine connection with your audience. Be honest about your brand's values, mission, and any challenges you may face.

4. **Customer Feedback and Reviews**: Actively listen to customer feedback and promptly address any concerns or issues. Encourage customers to leave reviews and testimonials, as positive reviews can significantly enhance your brand reputation. Use feedback as an opportunity for improvement and continuously strive to exceed customer expectations.

5. **Social Responsibility**: Engage in socially responsible initiatives that align with your brand values. Support causes that resonate with your target audience and communicate your commitment to making a positive impact. Demonstrating social responsibility can enhance your brand reputation and attract socially conscious customers.

6. **Monitor and Respond to Online Conversations**: Keep a close eye on online conversations about your brand. Monitor social media channels, review websites, and industry forums to stay informed about what people are saying. Respond promptly and professionally to any negative feedback or complaints.

7. **Build Relationships with Influencers**: Collaborate with influencers and industry experts who align with your brand values. Cultivate relationships with them to leverage their reach and credibility to enhance your brand reputation. Influencers can help amplify your message and expand your brand's visibility.

8. **Consistent Quality and Innovation**: Maintain a high-quality standard in your products or services and continuously innovate to stay ahead of the competition. Consistency in delivering quality and staying at the forefront of your industry contributes to a positive brand reputation.

Remember, building a positive brand reputation takes time and effort. It requires consistently delivering exceptional customer experiences, maintaining transparency, and actively managing your brand's online presence. Investing in your brand reputation can create a strong foundation for success, differentiate yourself from the competition, and cultivate long-term customer loyalty.

In conclusion, a positive brand reputation is a valuable asset that can significantly impact a company's success. It builds trust, fosters customer loyalty, attracts new customers, provides a competitive advantage, and enhances crisis resilience. By implementing strategies to develop and maintain a positive brand reputation, businesses can establish themselves as trusted and reputable leaders in their industry.

4. Competitive Advantage

In today's competitive business landscape, customer support can be a key differentiating factor. Companies that excel in providing timely and efficient customer support stand out from their competitors. Customers are more likely to choose a company that offers reliable and responsive support over its competitors. This gives the company a competitive edge and increases its chances of success.

The Power of Competitive Advantage

In today's highly competitive business landscape, finding ways to stand out is crucial for long-term success. One key element that can give companies an edge over their rivals is a solid competitive advantage. A competitive advantage sets a company apart and makes it more desirable to customers than its competitors. It can be the key to attracting and retaining customers, driving growth, and achieving business success.

What is Competitive Advantage?

Competitive advantage refers to the unique strengths and capabilities that allow a company to outperform its competitors. It is why customers choose one company's products or services over another. A competitive advantage can take various forms, including:

1. Cost Leadership

One common type of competitive advantage is cost leadership. This means that a company can produce and deliver its products or services at a lower cost than its competitors while maintaining acceptable quality. By operating more efficiently, streamlining processes, and leveraging economies of scale, companies with cost leadership can offer lower prices to customers, making them more attractive in the market.

2. Differentiation

Another type of competitive advantage is differentiation. Differentiation means offering unique and superior products or services that stand out. This can be achieved through innovative features, excellent quality, exceptional customer service, or a strong brand image. Differentiation allows companies to command higher prices and build customer loyalty based on the perceived value they provide.

3. Focus

A focus strategy involves targeting a specific market segment or niche and tailoring products or services to meet that segment's specific needs and preferences. By focusing on a particular customer group or geographic area, companies can develop deep expertise and better serve the needs of their target market. This focused approach allows companies to compete effectively in a smaller, specialized market where larger competitors may not have the same understanding or capability.

The Benefits of Competitive Advantage

Having a competitive advantage can bring numerous benefits to a company, including:

1. Increased Customer Attraction and Retention

A solid competitive advantage makes a company more desirable to customers. Whether it's offering lower prices, unique features, or specialized expertise, customers are more likely to choose a company that stands out from the competition. Moreover, a competitive advantage can help build customer loyalty, as customers recognize the value and benefits they receive from the company's products or services.

2. Higher Profitability

Companies with a competitive advantage often enjoy higher profitability. Cost leadership allows for higher profit margins, as lower production costs enable companies to maintain healthy profit levels even with lower prices. Differentiation and focus strategies can also lead to higher profitability by commanding premium prices and reducing the need for heavy price competition.

3. Market Leadership

A strong competitive advantage can help a company establish itself as a market leader. A company can gain a significant market share by consistently outperforming competitors and meeting customer needs better than anyone else. Market leadership brings numerous benefits, such as greater bargaining power with suppliers, increased brand recognition, and the ability to shape industry trends and standards.

4. Business Growth and Expansion

Competitive advantage can be a catalyst for business growth and expansion. As a company attracts more customers and gains market share, it can generate higher revenues and reinvest in further innovation, marketing, and expansion efforts. A solid competitive advantage also positions a company well for entering new markets or expanding its product or service offerings, as customers already recognize its superiority over competitors.

5. Sustainability

A sustainable competitive advantage can be maintained over the long term and withstand the challenges posed by competitors. By continuously investing in innovation, operational efficiency, and customer relationships, companies can build a competitive advantage that is difficult for competitors to replicate. Sustainability is critical for maintaining a solid market position and weathering changes in the business environment.

Strategies for Building and Sustaining Competitive Advantage

Building and sustaining a competitive advantage requires a strategic approach and ongoing efforts. Here are some strategies that can help companies establish and maintain their competitive edge:

1. Continuous Innovation

Innovation is essential for staying ahead and maintaining a competitive advantage. Companies should invest in research and development, regularly evaluate customer needs, and strive to bring new and improved products or services. Companies can offer unique and superior solutions that keep customers returning by continuously innovating.

2. Focus on Customer Experience

Delivering exceptional customer experiences is a powerful way to differentiate from competitors. By understanding customer needs, providing personalized interactions, and going above and beyond to exceed expectations, companies can build strong relationships and foster customer loyalty. Positive customer experiences become a part of a company's competitive advantage, as customers value the superior service they receive.

3. Operational Excellence

Operational efficiency and excellence can contribute to cost leadership and differentiation. Companies can lower costs while maintaining quality by optimizing processes, reducing waste, and improving productivity. This allows for competitive pricing or higher profit margins, depending on the company's strategy. Operational excellence enables companies to deliver products or services more efficiently and reliably than competitors.

4. Strong Branding and Marketing

Building a solid brand and effectively marketing it can help companies differentiate themselves from competitors. By clearly communicating their products' or services' unique value proposition and benefits, companies can attract customers who align with their brand values. A strong brand image and reputation can create a perception of superiority and trust, further enhancing the competitive advantage.

5. Continuous Learning and Adaptation

Companies must be agile and adaptable in a rapidly changing business environment to maintain their competitive advantage. This involves continuously learning about industry trends, customer preferences, and emerging technologies. By staying ahead of the curve and proactively adjusting strategies and offerings, companies can respond to market shifts and evolving customer needs, ensuring their competitive advantage remains relevant.

In conclusion, a solid competitive advantage is vital for companies seeking long-term success and growth. Whether through cost leadership, differentiation, or a focus strategy, a competitive advantage allows companies to attract and retain customers, achieve higher profitability, establish market leadership, and drive business expansion. By strategically investing in innovation, customer experience, operational excellence, branding, and continuous learning, companies can build and sustain their competitive advantage, positioning themselves for ongoing success in a competitive marketplace.

Remember, a competitive advantage is not static but requires ongoing effort and adaptation. Companies must continually evaluate their strategies, monitor the competitive landscape, and evolve to maintain their edge. With a well-defined and effectively executed competitive advantage, businesses can thrive and flourish in today's dynamic business environment.

5. Customer Retention

Timely and efficient customer support is vital for customer retention. Customers expect a prompt and satisfactory resolution when they encounter issues or have questions. If their concerns are not addressed promptly, they may become frustrated and seek alternatives. However, when companies prioritize timely and efficient customer support, it helps retain existing customers and prevent customer churn.

The Power of Customer Retention: Building Long-Term Success

Customer retention is a crucial aspect of business success. When companies focus on retaining their existing customers, they can reap numerous benefits, such as increased revenue, brand loyalty, and a competitive edge in the market. In this blog post, we will explore the importance of customer retention and discuss practical strategies to build long-term customer relationships.

Why is Customer Retention Important?

1. **Increased Revenue**: Retaining existing customers is more cost-effective than acquiring new ones. Studies have shown that attracting a new customer can cost up to five times more than retaining an existing one. By focusing on customer retention, businesses can maximize their revenue by fostering repeat purchases and customer loyalty.
2. **Brand Loyalty and Advocacy**: Loyal customers are likelier to become brand advocates. They continue to purchase products or services and recommend the brand to others. Positive word-of-mouth from loyal customers can significantly impact a company's reputation and attract new customers.
3. **Competitive Advantage**: Customer retention provides a competitive edge in today's competitive market. Companies prioritizing building solid customer relationships are likelier to differentiate themselves from competitors. Customers are more

likely to choose a brand they trust and have had positive experiences with, even if similar offerings are available elsewhere.

4. **Higher Customer Lifetime Value**: Customers who stay loyal to a brand tend to have higher lifetime value (CLV). They not only make repeat purchases but also have a higher likelihood of trying new products or services offered by the company. Their increased CLV translates into higher profitability for the business.

Strategies for Successful Customer Retention

Now that we understand the importance of customer retention, let's explore some practical strategies to build and maintain long-term customer relationships:

1. Provide Exceptional Customer Service

Exceptional customer service is the foundation of successful customer retention. When customers encounter issues or have questions, prompt and efficient support can make all the difference. By prioritizing customer satisfaction and investing in well-trained support teams, companies can build customer trust and loyalty.

2. Personalize the Customer Experience

Tailoring the customer experience to individual preferences can create a sense of personal connection and increase customer loyalty. Use customer data and insights to provide customized recommendations, exclusive offers, and personalized communication. Businesses can foster long-term relationships by showing genuine interest in customers' needs and preferences.

3. Engage Customers Through Communication

Regular and meaningful communication with customers is essential for nurturing long-term relationships. Stay connected with email newsletters, social media updates, and personalized follow-ups. Share valuable information, product updates, and special offers to keep customers engaged and remind them of the value your brand provides.

4. Implement a Customer Loyalty Program

Customer loyalty programs are practical tools for fostering customer retention. By offering rewards, discounts, or exclusive perks to loyal customers, businesses can incentivize repeat purchases and strengthen the bond with their customer base. Loyalty programs encourage ongoing engagement and create a sense of appreciation and exclusivity.

5. Seek and Act on Customer Feedback

Listening to customer feedback is vital for identifying areas of improvement and strengthening customer relationships. Regularly collect feedback through surveys, reviews, and customer support interactions. Analyze the feedback and take appropriate actions to address concerns and enhance the customer experience. By actively involving customers in the improvement process, businesses can show that their opinions are valued.

6. Continuously Innovate and Adapt

To retain customers, businesses must continuously innovate and adapt to evolving customer needs. Stay ahead of the competition by regularly introducing new products, features, or services that meet customers' changing expectations. Businesses can keep customers engaged and loyal by demonstrating a commitment to innovation and consistently delivering value.

7. Build Emotional Connections

Customers are more likely to stay loyal to brands that evoke positive emotions. Focus on building emotional connections through storytelling, brand values, and customer-centric experiences. When customers feel emotionally connected to a brand, they are likelier to remain loyal and advocate for it.

Conclusion

Customer retention is a critical component of long-term business success. Businesses can benefit from increased revenue, brand loyalty, and competitive advantage by prioritizing the retention of existing customers. Companies can build and maintain strong customer relationships through exceptional customer service, personalized experiences, effective communication, loyalty programs, customer feedback, continuous innovation, and emotional connections.

Remember, customer retention requires ongoing effort and dedication. Regularly review and refine your customer retention strategies based on customer feedback and changing market dynamics. By investing in customer retention, businesses can create a solid foundation for growth and thrive in today's competitive business landscape.

Conclusion

In conclusion, timely and efficient customer support is paramount for businesses. It contributes to customer satisfaction, loyalty, brand reputation, competitive advantage, and retention. Investing in a robust customer support system and ensuring efficient response times can significantly benefit a company and its overall success.

FUTURE-PROOFING YOUR BUSINESS: STAYING UPDATED

Joining tech-forward SMB communities

In today's digital age, small and medium-sized businesses (SMBs) increasingly embrace technology to gain a competitive edge and drive growth. Joining tech-forward SMB communities can be an excellent way for entrepreneurs and business owners to connect, collaborate, and stay up-to-date with the latest trends and innovations.

Benefits of joining tech-forward SMB communities

1. **Networking opportunities**: Tech-forward SMB communities provide a platform for like-minded individuals to connect and build professional relationships. By joining these communities, business owners can expand their network, meet potential partners or clients, and exchange ideas with industry peers.

2. **Access to knowledge and resources**: Being part of a tech-forward SMB community grants access to a wealth of knowledge and resources. Community members often share valuable insights, best practices, and tips for leveraging technology to enhance business operations. Additionally, these communities may provide access to exclusive educational materials, webinars, and workshops.

3. **Collaboration and partnerships**: Joining tech-forward SMB communities opens doors to collaboration and teamwork. Businesses can find opportunities to collaborate on projects, co-create products or services, and leverage each other's expertise.

Partnerships within these communities can lead to increased innovation, expanded market reach, and shared resources.

4. **Staying updated with industry trends**: The tech landscape constantly evolves, and SMBs must stay updated to remain competitive. Tech-forward SMB communities are a hub for visiting and informing about the latest industry trends, emerging technologies, and market insights. Through discussions, events, and knowledge sharing, community members can stay ahead of the curve and adapt their strategies accordingly.

How to join tech-forward SMB communities

1. **Research and identify relevant communities**: Start by researching and identifying tech-forward SMB communities that align with your industry, interests, and goals. Look for online communities, industry forums, social media groups, or local meetup groups that cater to SMBs with a focus on technology.

2. **Engage and participate**: Once you find suitable communities, actively engage and participate in discussions. Contribute your insights, ask questions, and share your experiences. Building a presence and establishing yourself as a valuable member will help you make the most of these communities.

3. **Attend events and webinars**: Many tech-forward SMB communities organize events, webinars, and workshops. Make an effort to attend these sessions to learn from industry experts, gain new perspectives, and connect with fellow members. These events also provide opportunities for networking and collaboration.

4. **Contribute and give back**: As you benefit from the tech-forward SMB community, remember to contribute and give back. Share your knowledge, offer help to others, and actively support fellow members. By being an active contributor, you can strengthen your reputation and build lasting relationships within the community.

Joining tech-forward SMB communities can provide immense value for entrepreneurs and business owners who embrace technology as a catalyst for growth. Connecting with like-minded individuals, accessing valuable resources, and staying updated with industry trends can position your business for success in the ever-evolving digital landscape.

CONCLUSION:

THE DIGITAL TRANSFORMATION JOURNEY

Embracing the continuous evolution of technology

In today's fast-paced digital landscape, small and medium-sized businesses (SMBs) must embrace the continuous evolution of technology. By doing so, SMBs can stay competitive, adapt to changing market trends, and unlock new growth opportunities. Here are some critical strategies for SMBs to embrace the continuous evolution of technology:

1. Stay Informed and Educated

To effectively embrace the continuous evolution of technology, SMBs need to stay informed about the latest trends, advancements, and innovations in their industry. This can be achieved by regularly reading technology blogs, attending industry conferences, and participating in webinars or workshops. Investing in ongoing employee training and development programs can ensure your team has the necessary skills and knowledge to leverage emerging technologies.

2. Foster a Culture of Innovation

Creating a culture of innovation within your organization is essential for embracing the continuous evolution of technology. Encourage your employees to think creatively, experiment with new technologies, and share their ideas for improving processes and products. Establishing cross-functional teams and providing them with the resources and freedom to explore innovative solutions can lead to breakthroughs and keep your business at the forefront of technological advancements.

3. Embrace Cloud Computing

Cloud computing has revolutionized businesses' operations, providing scalability, flexibility, and cost-efficiency. By embracing cloud computing, SMBs can streamline operations, enhance collaboration, and leverage powerful computing resources without significant upfront investments. Whether adopting cloud-based productivity tools, migrating to cloud storage solutions, or utilizing cloud-based software applications, embracing the cloud can enable SMBs to adapt quickly to changing technology landscapes.

4. Leverage Data Analytics

Data is a valuable asset for SMBs, and leveraging data analytics can unlock valuable insights and drive informed decision-making. Implementing robust data analytics tools and processes can help SMBs understand customer behavior, identify market trends, and optimize business operations. By leveraging data analytics, SMBs can make data-driven decisions, personalize customer experiences, and gain a competitive edge in the market.

5. Embrace Agile Methodologies

Agile methodologies, such as Agile project management and DevOps, enable SMBs to adapt quickly to changing technology requirements and deliver value to customers more efficiently. Embracing Agile methodologies involves breaking down projects into manageable tasks, fostering cross-functional collaboration, and embracing iterative development and continuous delivery practices. By adopting Agile methods, SMBs can accelerate time-to-market, improve product quality, and respond effectively to customer feedback and changing market demands.

The Power of Agile Methodology

In today's rapidly changing business landscape, agility is critical to success. This is especially true when it comes to technology and software development. Agile methodology has emerged as a powerful approach that allows small and medium-sized businesses (SMBs) to adapt quickly to changing technology requirements and deliver customer value more efficiently.

What is Agile Methodology?

Agile methodology is a collaborative and iterative project management and software development approach. It emphasizes flexibility, adaptability, and customer collaboration throughout the development process. Unlike traditional waterfall methods, which follow a linear and sequential approach, Agile methodology breaks down projects into manageable tasks and focuses on delivering working software in short iterations called sprints.

The Benefits of Agile Methodology for SMBs

1. Faster Time-to-Market

Agile methodology enables SMBs to accelerate their time-to-market by delivering working software in frequent iterations. This allows businesses to release valuable features and functionalities to customers earlier, gaining a competitive edge in the market. With Agile, SMBs can respond quickly to customer feedback and changing market demands, ensuring their products and services remain relevant and competitive.

2. Improved Product Quality

Through its iterative and collaborative nature, Agile methodology promotes continuous testing, feedback, and refinement. This results in improved product quality as issues and bugs are identified and addressed early in development. By embracing Agile, SMBs can ensure that their software meets customer expectations, leading to higher customer satisfaction and loyalty.

3. Enhanced Customer Collaboration

Agile methodology places a strong emphasis on customer collaboration throughout the development process. By involving customers early and frequently, SMBs can gain valuable insights and feedback, ensuring their products align with customer needs and preferences. This customer-centric approach allows SMBs to deliver solutions that meet customer expectations, enhancing customer satisfaction and fostering long-term relationships.

4. Increased Team Collaboration and Empowerment

Agile methodology promotes cross-functional collaboration and self-organizing teams. By breaking down projects into manageable tasks and fostering cooperation, SMBs can empower their teams to take ownership and make decisions, increasing team productivity and motivation. This collaborative environment also encourages knowledge sharing and innovation, driving continuous improvement within the organization.

5. Adaptability to Changing Requirements

In today's dynamic business environment, requirements can change rapidly. Agile methodology embraces change and allows SMBs to adapt quickly to evolving customer needs and market trends. Through its iterative and incremental approach, Agile enables SMBs to reprioritize and adjust project requirements based on feedback and changing circumstances, ensuring that the final product meets the most current needs of the business and its customers.

Getting Started with Agile Methodology

Implementing Agile methodology requires a shift in mindset and a commitment to collaboration and adaptability. SMBs can start by training their teams on Agile principles and practices, establishing cross-functional teams, and adopting Agile project management tools. Creating a supportive and empowering work culture that encourages experimentation, learning, and continuous improvement is also essential.

In conclusion, Agile methodology significantly benefits SMBs navigating the ever-changing technology landscape. By embracing Agile, SMBs can accelerate their time-to-market, improve product quality, enhance customer collaboration, and adapt to changing requirements. This approach empowers SMBs to stay competitive, deliver customer value, and thrive in the digital age.

Remember, agility is not just a methodology – it's a mindset that enables SMBs to embrace the continuous evolution of technology.

By following these strategies, SMBs can embrace the continuous evolution of technology and position themselves for long-term success in the digital age. Embracing technology enables SMBs to stay competitive, drive innovation, and capitalize on emerging opportunities in the ever-evolving technology landscape.

The potential of SMBs in the tech-driven era

Small and medium-sized businesses (SMBs) have always played a crucial role in the economy, but their potential for growth and success in today's tech-driven era has reached new heights. With advancements in technology and the increasing accessibility of digital tools, SMBs now have the opportunity to thrive and compete with larger enterprises on a global scale.

One of the critical advantages that technology offers SMBs is the ability to level the playing field. In the past, limited resources and budget constraints may have hindered the growth of small businesses. However, with the rise of cloud computing, artificial intelligence, and automation, SMBs can now access the tools and technologies that were once only available to large corporations. This enables them to streamline operations, improve efficiency, and deliver products and services more effectively.

Additionally, technology has revolutionized the way SMBs interact with their customers. With the advent of social media, online marketplaces, and e-commerce platforms, SMBs can reach a wider audience and target specific customer segments with precision. Digital marketing strategies, such as search engine optimization and targeted advertising, allow SMBs to compete for visibility and cost-effectively attract customers. Furthermore, customer relationship management (CRM) systems and data analytics provide valuable insights into consumer behavior, enabling SMBs to personalize their offerings and enhance customer satisfaction.

Collaboration and innovation are also enhanced in the tech-driven era. SMBs can now leverage remote work tools, project management software, and communication platforms to collaborate with employees, partners, and clients across geographical boundaries. This opens up opportunities for outsourcing, partnerships, and accessing a global talent pool. Moreover, SMBs can tap into the vast collection of online knowledge and resources, including online communities, forums, and educational platforms, to continuously learn, innovate, and stay ahead of the competition.

However, it is essential to acknowledge the challenges that SMBs may face in embracing technology. Limited technological expertise, cybersecurity risks, and the need for ongoing investments in technology infrastructure can pose hurdles. SMBS must invest in digital skills training, seek guidance from technology experts, and implement robust security measures to mitigate these challenges and fully leverage the potential of technology.

In conclusion, the tech-driven era presents immense opportunities for SMBs to grow, innovate, and thrive. By harnessing the power of technology, SMBs can overcome traditional barriers, reach new markets, and deliver exceptional products and services. Embracing technology is no longer a luxury but a necessity for SMBs to remain competitive and realize their full potential in today's digital landscape.

THE END

www.ingramcontent.com/pod-product-compliance
Lightning Source LLC
Chambersburg PA
CBHW070918260726

48661CB00003B/749